Gloria Gemma's Forever in Our Hearts

a collection of stories & memories

VOLUME ONE

edited by
SUSAN LATAILLE

**Gloria Gemma's Forever in Our Hearts:
A Collection of Stories & Memories, Volume One**
Copyright © 2023 Susan Lataille

Produced and printed by Stillwater River Publications.
All rights reserved. Written and produced in the
United States of America. This book may not be reproduced
or sold in any form without the expressed, written
permission of the author(s) and publisher.

First Stillwater River Publications Edition

ISBN: 978-1-960505-69-9

1 2 3 4 5 6 7 8 9 10
Edited by Susan Lataille.
Cover & interior book design by Matthew St. Jean.
Published by Stillwater River Publications,
West Warwick, RI, USA.

*The views and opinions expressed
in this book are solely those of the authors
and do not necessarily reflect the views
and opinions of the publisher.*

GLORIA GEMMA'S

FOREVER IN OUR HEARTS

Contents

Introduction   *vii*
About the Authors   *xi*

1. Be Aware of the Butterflies   *Christina Pirolli*   1
2. The "C" Word   *Jennifer Aracely Berrio Ortiz*   16
3. The Last Year   *Leslie Tordoff*   51
4. Heaven Called You Home   *Brittney L. D'Arezzo*   64
5. She Wore It Well   *Lisa Bastien*   80
6. From Mom to Guardian Angel   *Melissa Bouchard*   96
7. In Every Sense of the Word   *Sara Vazquez*   112
8. Wonder.   *Eduardo Vazquez Jr.*   128
9. Not Yet, Mom   *Jeanette Simoes*   144
10. A Mother's Love   *Arthur Parise Jr.*   160

Introduction

Grief is a unique and often muddy creature. It is defined as "deep sorrow, especially that caused by someone's death," but grief can be more than an emotion; it can impact our physical, behavioral, and spiritual wellbeing. Some people deal with their loss and move forward, while others seem perpetually fixed in a state of mourning, unable to experience true happiness—even years after their loss. Still, there are those people who choose to turn their proverbial backs on their grief, ignoring and suppressing any feelings of distress.

The Gloria Gemma Foundation understands the many faces of grief. Over the years, its staff and core volunteers have provided support to families through the passing of their loved ones, through the grieving process and beyond.

Experts claim there are five stages of grief: denial, anger, bargaining, depression, and acceptance, and these emotions surface at any time, in any order. Maybe hope and remembrance should also be added to the list. We all hope our loved ones who've passed are in a place of abounding love and joy with no pain—their ailments all cured. And we remember our loved ones, often reminiscing with other family members and friends. It is keeping their loved ones' memories alive so those left behind can truly heal.

That is why the Sharing Your Loved One's Story Group was born. Susan Lataille, a certified grief coach, used writing as a tool to help her through the loss of her son. Susan wrote about her son in the book *Shining Your Light on Grief Anthology,* and invited others who lost loved ones to be contributing authors. Writing their loved ones' story gave the writers an opportunity to truly grieve and heal.

The Foundation recognized the need for this type of program; however, this is not the first book to which people connected to the Foundation have been contributing authors. The first book the Foundation published in 2010 was *Journey from Despair to Hope,* in which cancer survivors and caretakers wrote about their individual journeys, providing healing for all the participants as they worked through the trauma of cancer as a group. They leaned on one another, they supported each other, and lasting friendships were made.

Sharing Your Loved One's Story Group is comprised of survivors connected to the Foundation's programs who have lost family members or family members of cancer patients whom the Foundation has supported through the passing of their loved ones. Regardless of how these ten people came to us, they are bonded by the loss of people they loved, and they are healing through sharing their stories.

We hope this book will inspire you to have hope and to shine your light on grief.

About the Authors

Christina Pirolli

Be Aware of the Butterflies

Be Aware of the Butterflies is the story of five of my hardest years. It tells of the journey of losing three of the most important people in my life, my mom, my friend Dana, and my dad to cancer. Although it is a story rooted in loss, sadness, and struggle, it truly is a story of love, learning, and strength. It was in my darkest moments that I was able to discover who I really am and embrace life after so much loss. Through heartache, tears, and a little laughter *Be Aware of the Butterflies* is the story of life after loss.

I wanted to tell my story initially as a way to honor the ones I loved and lost. Each one of them was incredible in so many aspects and each of their journeys in their own way helped to shape me into the person I am today. But what started as a way for me to tell their stories ultimately turned into a path for healing. Telling their stories allowed me to also share the message that no matter how devastating a hand we are dealt, life does indeed go on. I grew to understand that I needed to tell this story not just for me and my loved ones, but for anyone out there who is grieving to let them know it will get better.

I am currently living in Providence, RI with my parents' dog Halsey. I work as a personal trainer and nutrition coach. I am passionate about helping others become their strongest and healthiest selves. When I'm not in the gym, I love to spend time outside traveling and eating. I am working to live life to the fullest and make as many memories as I can along the way.

Jennifer Aracely Berrio Ortiz

The "C" Word

This is a story about the best mother in the world. I'm sure most daughters feel this way about their mothers but read all about my Mami in my chapter. My mom had me at the age of seventeen. I had forty-three amazing years of being her daughter, her Queen. We had and continue to have an extremely strong bond. When I was twenty-five years old, I quit my job at a salon. My mom believed in me more than myself. She refinanced the house and gave me the money to open my own shop in 2004. Nineteen years later I am still a small business owner of Executive Cuts at 15 Peck St., Downtown Providence, RI 02903. The way cancer has run rampant through my family has altered our lives completely. I used to think it couldn't get worse, but I no longer think that. It can always get worse.

Writing has propelled my grief in such a cathartic way. Reevaluating my life, my relationship with family and friends. Learning who loves me unconditionally the way my Ma used too. Not many do. My circle has gotten smaller and smaller but it's about quality not quantity. I wanted to share our story to help others try to get through their grief. Grief is so fluid. I'm only forty-two weeks into living without my mother. I am relearning who I am now. She made me such a strong woman. The way life continues to happen without her feels surreal. There are so many moments I want to run and tell her some news and it hits like a ton of bricks. She's not here! She always wanted me to continue my education. Now that I am dual-licensed, she cannot rejoice with me, but I know she sees all my and all her loved ones' accomplishments. She was EVERYONE'S Wela after all.

In my story, I write about a beautiful soul we called Nurse Rachel. Unfortunately, she will not have the chance to read about herself. Rachel, I hope my mom was waiting for you. The beautiful girls you left behind, Noel and Joy, have my devoted support. May you both rest in eternal peace.

Rachael Lynne Cassidy, January 10, 1975 – June 9, 2023

Connect with Jennifer:
Cell phone: 401-419-0546
Email: executivecuts2014@gmail.com

Leslie Tordoff

The Last Year

This was and will be the hardest time of my existence. It's the story of how the love of my life, my guy, was taken unfairly away from me by cancer. Leaving me to live the rest of my days without him physically. It's about seeing a strong man, who I love dearly, decline in health and helping him the best way I knew how. To learn there is life and happiness after a massive loss and coming to terms with the struggles of grief.

I'm an introvert and it's hard for me to share my feelings, never mind writing them down. I took this opportunity to help me process my feelings and to learn how to express myself through writing. It hasn't been easy, but it gave me a state of peace. I hope that by sharing my story with others who are in a struggling stage of grief, that they can feel they aren't alone, and maybe if they see I can do it, they can do it too.

I'm a woman who misses her soulmate every day. I had to relearn how to live and to find happiness on my own after his passing. I enjoy gardening, spin class, volunteering through Gloria Gemma Breast Cancer Resource Foundation, and reading. I'm very passionate about my career, which helps keep me on track obtaining my goals. My family is the light of my life and I'm so fortunate to have them. They bring me so much joy and happiness watching each one of them grow and thrive. I love them dearly.

Brittney L. D'Arezzo

Heaven Called You Home

My story is about someone who was my best friend, an amazing mother, wife, etc… This was someone who I was so proud to call my mom. My mom and I had a bond like no other. She had me at twenty-four, so she was a younger mom. I was blessed to have had her for thirty years, but in reality we both were robbed of time. No matter how old you are in life, a daughter is never prepared to lose their mother. My mom was my biggest cheerleader in life, and the one person who I could always count on. My mom was the one person who supported me, and believed in me more than I believed in myself. Reading this story, it will make you realize how quickly life can change, and to enjoy your life to the fullest. I never thought someone who I loved with my whole heart would have been diagnosed with the big C word. This chapter teaches you and reminds you to show your loved ones how much you love them, and if you do have a loved one who was diagnosed with cancer you are not alone. It is a timeline of her childhood life through her present life until she passed away on July 2nd, 2023.

I wanted to share my story with the world for many reasons. I want the world to know how wonderful of a person my mom was, and how strong she really was. It has been eleven months since losing my mom, and I still feel so lost and hold so many emotions as I am still grieving. After losing my mom, nothing has been easy. I hit rock bottom, but I am slowly getting back on my feet. My mom was young when she passed, and I had made a promise to my mom that her spirit would live on forever so that is exactly what I am doing by writing about her journey. Not only did I promise my mom that we would keep her spirit alive, but the cancer she was diagnosed with that you are about to read about unfortunately is not curable. I wanted to write about her journey and be a voice for those who are battling this cancer and any cancer to hope one day there will be a cure. Until then we as the family have to be the advocate to keep fighting and not give up hope. That was one thing my mom always told me, "Always have hope, never stop fighting, but most of all, pray."

I am thirty years old and come from Rhode Island. I have a big heart and love to help others. I am an independent single woman, who has nephews and a niece that I love like my own. I wish for nothing more than to have my mom read this story, and know how much she was loved not only by me but all those who knew her.

Lisa Bastien

You Wore it Well

Donna was my sister and my everything to me, and I would do anything for her. I wrote this story from my heart and how I remember her life through my eyes.

I tell my story because there are thousands of people living who share this same experience. I want to make sure Donna's story doesn't get lost. Even after she was diagnosed, her personality shined through. She continued to smile, to care for those around her, and to be grateful for every day. She wore it well.

I am a product of my upbringing. I come from a large family and we didn't have much but we had each other. I am proud of who I am and what I have overcome and a lot of that is because of my sister, Donna. I would not be who I am if not for her.

Melissa Bouchard

From Mom to Guardian Angel

My chapter is not only about who my mom was as a person but also who she is as my guardian angel through life and through my own journey with cancer. Throughout my life since my mom's passing, I have felt her presence all around me, showing signs when I needed it the most. In the 90's, they didn't have the type of support they do now for kids that lose their parents too early. Since I didn't trust going to a therapist, I had to rely on my support system, which was a mix of family and friends, to get me through my worst days as I learned how to live without my mom.

It's so hard losing a loved one at any age and I hope that this can help those who are going through it at such a young age. Social media wasn't what it is today so I didn't have that outlet to share my mom's story and to honor her memory. I've always wanted a way to share her story, so when the Gloria Gemma Foundation posted about this project, I was really excited. I'm so happy to be given this opportunity to share my mom's story and to continue to keep her memory alive.

My name is Melissa Bouchard and I grew up in Cranston, RI. My husband and I have been together for seventeen years and we just celebrated our ten-year wedding anniversary in March. We have a beautiful eight-year-old daughter who is truly the love of our lives and is so beautiful inside and out. I graduated from JWU in 2008 with a bachelor's degree in business management and after many years in the restaurant business, I left and joined the corporate world. September will mark eight years that I've worked for my current employer, Schneider Electric. I was diagnosed with stage II triple-negative breast cancer in October of 2020 and after chemo, radiation, and many surgeries, I was able to celebrate being two years cancer-free in April.

Sara Melissa Vazquez

In Every Sense of the Word

This is the journey of the warrior, Elizabeth, descendant of la Isla del Encanto. She would go on to master and share her gifts with the world, forging three of her very own, to bestow upon the Island of Rhode. Her second born, she would call Sara Melissa Vazquez, first of her name. The center of her power of three and as time would have it, they would multiply, making her forces unstoppable.

I wanted to write to honor my mother and because it has served as an outlet for me. I have always been reluctant and maybe even timid to share any of my work with anyone outside of my circle. It comes as no surprise that my mom found a way to bring me the courage or that my first published work would be of me telling her story through my lens. It is very fitting and humorous. She always loved to tell a story. She could find any moment where one of her stories would apply or enhance. She knew what she knew too because nothing has been more gratifying and healing than being able to read the stories she left in writing and print. You see, she is still teaching lessons here. I plan to take heed and do the same for my boys and for anyone that may receive anything beneficial from the words that I write.

In the meantime, I will continue my work as a mother and advocate for my children and for the individuals I serve in the healthcare field. When I have the luxury of carving out some "me" time, I love to balance myself through travel. I would also say that writing, reading and being a voice to injustice is a hard number two.

Eduardo Vazquez Jr.

Wonder.

This chapter involves my thoughts and feelings regarding the loss of my mother, Elizabeth Cardona and trying to process that grief. I hope seeing the world the way she did will help answer some of my questions, stay connected with her, and begin healing. Sharing this story proved to be very difficult, but if I can even reach one person who feels similarly, then I'm happy and following in the footsteps of my mother.

My family and friends know me as Eddy. I was born in Providence, Rhode Island. I'm the youngest of three children and a momma's boy through and through. While I enjoy the occasional moment of solitude, I'm better known for my loud personality and all that it entails. Growing up I was definitely amongst the more extroverted. During my early years as an adult I moved to California, circa 2008. I consider myself to be "west coast living but east coast at heart." I love exploration and indulging in my creative side. I enjoy culture, traveling, and spending time with my family and friends, as well as writing, dancing, performing, and more. I usually write poetry but I do have a keen interest in one day writing short stories.

Jeanette Simoes

Mom, Not Yet

This story is about my mother and her fight with cancer; how she lived her life before and after cancer. I watched my mother go from this energetic vibrant person to one in pain, worried, and a sad person. I pictured my mother living until her nineties with great grandchildren. She had a beautiful life. In my lifetime I never imagined her life would end to breast cancer. I am grateful I spent thirty-seven years of my life with her. Toward the end, she said to me "be happy and be with the people who love you". I will forever follow those words until my last breath.

I wanted to share my story because I know the feeling of being lost without a loved one, with kind words it helps ease some of those sad days. Losing someone that completely understood you leaves a hole in your heart that no one can fill. I have been living with this for a few years. It hurts. With a hug, a glass of wine, and good conversation your mind drifts away from grief for a moment. Those moments away from grief are wonderful and I wanted my story to have that moment to whomever reads it. I believe life was never intended to be easy but to be always in the "moment." My mother's presence and grace were just that.

I am energetic, loving, caring and funny. I am a wife and a mother. I have a beautiful five-year-old son named Andre; he was diagnosed with autism three years ago and is non-verbal. He is the most beautiful little boy you would ever meet. He loves hugs, tickles, and kisses. He has brought me joy in my darkest times. I am beyond grateful for him. Three years ago I started working for The Fogarty Center, it was life changing for me, feeling more appreciated on the job and learning about adults and children with disabilities. They have helped me find resources and help for my son. I am happy they found me.

If you ever would like to connect with me, please email me at jeanetteking@yahoo.com.

Arthur Parise Jr.

A Mother's Love

My chapter follows the timeline of my life both before my mother's breast cancer diagnosis and after she passed away. Through this story you will grow to understand my personal relationship with my mother as well as how much she has impacted my life and helped me to become the man I am today.

I wanted to share my story to help those who may have recently lost a loved one to know that life does move forward and those we love will always be with us and are never really gone. I also wanted those who never had the chance to meet my mother get a glimpse of what kind of woman she was and the impact she had on my life.

I currently live in Downtown Providence with my boyfriend and am a kindergarten special education teacher. I run both in half-marathons and full marathons. My love of Star Wars continues to this day and I recently have gotten into bartending. I continue to be heavily involved in the Gloria Gemma Breast Cancer Foundation to continue my mother's legacy and help those affected by breast cancer.

Gloria Gemma's

Forever in Our Hearts

CHAPTER 1

Be Aware of the Butterflies

In Loving Memory of
Patricia A. Pirolli (June 18, 1948 – August 18, 2012)
Dana A. Cardillo (January 29, 1971 – November 16, 2015)
Anthony L. Pirolli (March 16, 1949 – September 29, 2017)

By Christina Pirolli

There are some moments in life that will forever be engrained in you. Some good. Some terrible. And no matter how hard you try to forget the horrible ones, you simply cannot. They become such a part of you that sometimes when you close your eyes the scene plays out like a movie. Except, when you open your eyes, the reality hits. It's not a movie. It did happen. It is real life.

For me, the day I learned of my mom's cancer diagnosis is one of those moments that will forever be stitched into my soul.

It was an ordinary Tuesday in February. I was lying on my sofa relaxing with my roommate. We were planning a trip for that April. It had been a few months since I left a toxic relationship and I was looking forward to embracing life. Little did I know that was all about to change.

It was all so ordinary. My leg propped up on the sofa back. The two of us laughing and joking as we looked at all of the tropical possibilities.

It was all so ordinary until my phone rang. It was my mom. Nothing strange there, we talked on the phone a lot. Her voice was calm and steady, "I have breast cancer."

It was as if time had stopped. Could she really be saying what she said? No! There's no way. Her voice steady, "did you hear me?"

There was no sense of urgency in her voice. No fear. No worry. It was as if she was calling to tell me what they ate for dinner that night.

In an instant I went from confusion to panic. Because as calm as she was, I, all of a sudden, could not breathe. How on earth could this be happening to my mom? My mom was truly the kindest person I knew and aside from not seeming possible it just wasn't fair.

It was all so surreal. In reality, the phone call lasted all of ten minutes. But in my mind an entire lifetime flashed by. In ten minutes my whole world felt like it was collapsing.

There's no way it could be cancer. No one in our family had had breast cancer. Yes, she was being treated for a cyst for a few months, but it was a cyst, not cancer. I mean surely the doctors would know the difference between a cyst and a malignant tumor.

With a whirlwind of thoughts swirling in my head I could finally take a breath big enough to quiver the words "Is it bad?"

With just as much calmness and even more confidence, my mom declared "I AM GOING TO BE FINE."

Although still paralyzed with fear and wanting to know more I clung to those six words.

I AM GOING TO BE FINE!

That phrase is something my mom repeated quite often over the next two years.

I still don't know if it was her genuinely optimistic nature or her nurturing desire to comfort us. My mom was always worried about taking care of everyone else and this situation was no different. No matter how bad things seemed I really hoped that she was correct. I needed everything to be fine because I needed my mom.

And so, we began our cancer journey.

There was the typical "routine" that most people battling cancer go through. Countless doctor's appointments. Endless lab work. Chemotherapy sessions. The horrible days following chemo. Surgery. Radiation. The good days sprinkled in.

And then there were the not so typical things. The things that made your heart stop. The things that made you question everything. The things that for a moment when you were by yourself made you think that maybe she was wrong. Maybe she wasn't going to be fine. An infected port. Septic shock. Medical induced coma. Weeks in the ICU. Heart rate crashing. Machines beeping and alarms sounding. Each one making your heart stop and your mind think it is not going to be fine.

But she was a fighter. She came back. And no matter how many steps backwards the journey took us she took ten steps forward with a strength I couldn't imagine.

She never complained. She never questioned why this was happening to her. She never doubted that she would be fine.

She would even humor me by trying all the things I was hoping would cure her. Wheatgrass shots. Every smoothie under the sun. Eliminating foods. Trips to Boston. Experimental drugs. You name it. If I thought it would help, I insisted we try it and she willingly complied without question.

I read so many books about cancer I lost count. Surely, somewhere in the thousands of pages I read, there was a cure. Surely, in the midst of all of those words, I was going to find the secret that was going to save my mom.

I would have done absolutely anything to make her better.

Despite my best efforts not to, I became angry.

Maybe my mom wasn't questioning the fairness of it all but I most certainly was. How could this be happening to someone so good? How come every bad thing that could be happening with cancer treatment was happening? Why couldn't she catch a break? Why couldn't there ever be one small glimmer of hope?

When things got rough, my mom would say "I give it to God."

When things got rough, I started to question if God even existed.

I never let on that I was angry. I kept it all to myself. Especially in front of my mom. I held it all in. To the outside world everything was fine.

I kept the messiness for when I was alone. I cried in the shower. I screamed when I was alone in my car. I coped in all the unhealthy ways. I'd go from the hospital to the bar. It was a cycle that kept me going and was a cycle that made me not have to think about what seemed like the inevitable.

Most of my friends didn't get it. It wasn't because they were insensitive. It was because they literally didn't understand. It was okay because I preferred to spend whatever time I wasn't with my mom with people who didn't know. I did things that, if even for a brief moment, would make me forget cancer existed. Some healthy; I started yoga. My time on the mat was an hour I could pretend life was normal. Some not so healthy; I drank a lot because that let me be numb to the reality of what was happening. This cycle of cancer life, yoga life, and bar life somehow gave me a balance and escape I was so desperately seeking.

As the cancer spread my mom continued to say she was going to be fine. It initially spread to her lungs but oddly enough that was the first time we ever had a glimmer of hope. We went to Boston where the doctor presented us with options of treatments we could try. It didn't matter to me that at this point she was so weak she could barely stand because there were options. For the first time in a long-time I started to think that she was right, everything was going to be fine. We had a few good months and then it all came crashing down. The cancer had spread to her brain. But just as quickly as we were brought down, we were brought back up. Radiation. Again. This time on her head. I clung back on to hope. It had appeared that the radiation was working until things became strange. My mom was forgetting words. She couldn't remember what she was trying to say. For the first time, my mom was scared. She tried to hide it. Tried to reassure me. But I could see it in her eyes.

It was a June afternoon. We were standing in the kitchen of my parents' house and I just knew that something was wrong. I called her doctor in Boston and he suggested we go to the emergency room. After a couple hours of testing and exams the doctor came in and he didn't have to say one word. I could just tell by his face it wasn't good. There were more metastatic spots on her brain in addition to swelling most likely from the radiation. On top of it, her kidney and liver function were declining which meant no more chemo. Her body just couldn't handle it anymore. It was the first time in almost two years that I cried in front of her. When my dad and aunt got to the hospital there were more tears. And, with only a slight glistening of tears, she looked at the three of us and reassured us she was going to be fine.

She stood by that for the next six weeks. No matter how many times or ways someone told her there were no other options she asserted she would be fine.

There were a few hospital stays within that time. Yet another birthday of hers was spent in one. There was a kind nurse I will forever be grateful to for bringing her a margarita, virgin of course, that she kept talking about. It wasn't all tears. We did have a few laughs. My normally quiet, never say a bad thing about anyone mom was no longer shy to give her opinion. She dropped some pearls of wisdom along the way as well, always prefacing them with "the point being is."

After the back-and-forth pattern that became a normal part of our life for the past two years we were going home for good.

Well, for two weeks. That's how much time they said we had left with her. Two weeks. I wanted a lifetime. But I would have settled for a few months. Two weeks was just unreasonable.

The plan for the day was that I would go to the hospital and wait for my mom to be discharged. My dad would wait at home for hospice to bring everything. My aunt would meet us at the house later that afternoon.

Two weeks.

I was trying to tell myself I could capture the lifetime I wanted into those two weeks. But the minute I stepped into her room I had a feeling I wouldn't get that time. She kept asking about a girl who had been in her room earlier asking if she was ready. She wasn't ready then, but she was ready now. It wouldn't seem alarming, it being a hospital, except no one dressed in all brown had been in her room to see if she was ready. Well at least no one that anyone else could see.

My aunt texted me to see how things were going, and it was in that moment I knew for certain we weren't going to have two weeks. My aunt said that the butterfly bush in her yard, the one that never attracted a single butterfly, was covered in them. As I read the words, my heart sank. The year before I had attended a health expo. While there I received a reiki treatment and, as it often happens, the practitioner picks up on things. He asked if my mom was living. She was, sick, but living. He said it was a female who had already passed and although he didn't know what it meant she was telling me to be aware of the butterflies. I had completely forgotten about that until I read that text from my aunt. And it was then that the reality of that simple statement came crashing down. Once again, I found myself unable to take a breath. I wasn't going to have two weeks with my mom. I was losing her that day. I never said anything to my aunt or my dad. Maybe I wanted them to think they had more time with her. Maybe I wanted to believe it for myself. And there we were on a bright and sunny August day taking my mom home.

It was a seamless transition. She didn't want hospice because she of course was going to be fine and didn't need it. I convinced her that they weren't going for her but to help me know how to take care of her.

When it came time to give her a dose of medicine, she became panicked and agitated and nothing we did could calm her down. I can still hear her crying that she wanted to go home. My dad trying to explain she was home. And me, already with the insight from earlier, knowing her house wasn't the home she was talking about. My mom, still strong in her faith, was telling us she wanted to go home to heaven.

We had to have her transported to the hospice facility that evening because we couldn't calm her. The nurse told us we weren't looking at two weeks but maybe two days. I didn't need her to tell me that but I was grateful I never had to say what I already knew in my heart.

Sadly, we didn't even get the two days. My mom died at 4:40 the next morning. August 18, 2012.

As she took her last breath, a piece of me died with her. And I said out loud the words I had been saying in my head for two years. IT'S NOT FAIR. I yelled and cried and held tight to my mom. It wasn't fair that she got sick and it most certainly wasn't fair that she suffered so much. It wasn't fair that a nurse, moments earlier, had expected me to tell her it was okay to go. It wasn't okay. And I wouldn't say it. I couldn't, which is something I still regret almost eleven years later. Why couldn't I just let her know after all the suffering it was okay for her to finally rest.

I can't go back and change that moment. And I know it was my love for her and my not wanting her to go that held me back. I would like to think she knew it was love and not selfishness that would not let me utter those words. That the only words I could scream with a heart wrenching scream were "It's not fair."

It wasn't. And if we are being honest there are still moments when I think it wasn't fair.

The few days and weeks after, I moved through life in a fog. I moved back into my apartment. I went to work. But life wasn't and would never be the same. I was angry that my mom couldn't have been one of the survivors. I was angry that I didn't have my mother and all of my friends had theirs. I was angry at God. I was angry at the world.

I was so angry I couldn't even fully appreciate the signs my mom was sending. The butterfly in the driveway of my parents' house that let my dad pick it up. The butterflies on one of the card options at the funeral home. The picture my friend Dana sent me from her trip which she postponed for my mom's funeral. A picture I still have to this day of a flower in her daughter's hand with a butterfly landing.

I saw them as signs but didn't let them start to heal me because it was much easier to be angry and bitter and think how unfair life had been.

I kept with my same healthy and unhealthy coping mechanisms. I dated men that I knew were not good for me. But I didn't care. I didn't want to be happy. I didn't want to live a good life without my mom here to see it.

So, I would just coast through, in a fog, living a surface level life. There were times I would pretend I was fine and things were good but would then rush home and curl into bed and cry.

I hated to sleep in the first couple of months because that meant I had to remember it was not a dream every time I woke up.

It was a few months later that I saw one of my mom's many last-day lessons play out. The husband of a friend lost his battle to cancer. He had two young children and it was heartbreaking to see them go through what I had just gone through. I was an adult. I had thirty-four years with my mom. Not enough years of course but more years than they had with their dad. They were just kids. My mom's first lesson to me, no matter how bad it seems, someone always has it worse.

That is also the moment I first got involved with the Gloria Gemma Foundation. They were hosting an art grief night for kids. Dana had thought it would be a good idea if we took all the kids in our life recently affected by cancer. I thought I was doing something for the kids but had no idea it was going to put me on the path to my own healing.

It was at the foundation that I saw for the first time I wasn't alone. Yes, there were people battling cancer, memories of people who had lost their battle, and those of us left behind but there was also hope. There was a hope that through it all you could still thrive. After that night, Dana and I would attend occasional events at the foundation together. We formed a team and walked in the Gloria Gemma 5K every year. A bittersweet tradition was started. Each year we would walk and then go out to eat. It was one of the first times I realized that happiness could rise from heartbreaking sadness.

For the longest time I had thought closing myself off to the world was my way to honor my mom. If she couldn't be here then I didn't deserve a good life. But by talking with people at the foundation I learned how backwards that was. My mom wouldn't have wanted me to waste my time here. She would have wanted me to make every moment count.

I started to shift away from my bad habits. Not all, I still purposely picked the worst guys, but that was a lesson to learn later. I slowly became more involved in yoga thanks to Dana and eventually loved it so much I became a certified yoga instructor.

I don't know if things would have turned around had I not had Dana. When people would ask how we met I would always say it was fate. And it was. We met the year before my mom was diagnosed. I was teaching kindergarten and one morning about a month after school started my principal knocked on my door. He had a favor to ask. Could he transfer a little girl from the other class into my room? She's cute, sweet, sadly her mom is fighting breast cancer and she was having a tough time. Without thinking, I said yes. And that is how Dana entered my life. I knew instantly that I liked her. I had a sense we would become friends. But I never knew how intertwined our lives would become because of cancer. And I never imagined that Dana would be pulling me out of the deepest hole because I would, only two years later, lose my mom. From when my mom was diagnosed, all through her sickness, until the moment she died, Dana was the only person outside of my family that got it. I never had to explain how I was feeling. She just knew. I never had to pretend around her. I could truly be myself.

So, when I say it was fate that Dana and I met, I mean it. I can't say for certain that I wouldn't have healed but it would have been many, many, years and more bad decisions down the road. It certainly wasn't easy making the choice to pull myself out of the darkness but I was learning that the alternative was even harder.

I began to see that living life wasn't dishonoring my mom but indeed honoring her in the best way that I could. Were there times that life sucked? Absolutely. Almost eleven years later and those moments still happen. The only difference now is it's easier to pull myself back. I don't dwell in those moments. I honor them and respect the grief but remind myself I can't live there because that's not living.

Slowly the things that initially brought tears to my eyes began to make me smile. Butterflies. Sunflowers. Chocolate. Margaritas.

Slowly I learned it was okay to be happy.

But more importantly, I learned it was okay to be sad. It was okay to cry no matter how much time had passed. It was okay to hate Mother's Day. It was okay to scream when I had an "oh I have to call my mom to tell her" moment, only to have the harsh realization I can't.

I learned there is no one right way to grieve. There's no stopping point. Grief will come and go and come again when you least expect it. And that's okay. It's okay to have a moment where you think life is unfair. But it's equally important to have the moments when you realize just how wonderful life actually is.

In my attempt to try to live a miserable life because my mom couldn't live hers, I lost the fact that that was the ultimate way to honor her. I needed to live my life to the fullest because she couldn't. I needed to do all the things she kept putting off because she was always caring for the needs of someone else. And in the moments that I get angry or want to complain about the stupidest thing, I remind myself that my mom never once complained. Even when she was in the worst pain I never once heard her say "Why me?" or complain in the slightest.

That was just who my mom was. I'm not exaggerating when I say she was the nicest person you could have known. Some may argue a little too nice, always putting the needs of others above her own. My mom wasn't one to throw around affection, but you never doubted how much she loved you. She was always a voice of reason, even if I didn't want to hear it. She was never one to boast or brag, and in those moments when she most certainly could have thrown an "I told you so" my way, she never did. My mom helped everyone she could. When I was grown and off to college and she could have been enjoying life on her terms, she took in her great niece and then two more and raised them as her own. The trips she had probably wanted to take turned into trips to Storyland and Santa's Village for the kids. My mom was selfless and caring and the very definition of unconditional love.

How could I not honor that?

I would like to say that my mom's battle with cancer was the last of it but sadly that's not the case. I had my own scare with cancer, an incidental finding on a routine appendectomy. I was fine. And I truly believe I was fine because I had a guardian angel who always believed everything was going to be fine. I also had an angel here, Dana, who would laugh with me when needed but would also let me cry too. She got it. She understood the fear. She understood the disbelief. She understood needing life to go on as normal.

Dana battled her cancer on and off all of the years I knew her. When we talk about strong women, Dana is at the top of the list. She truly lived life and made the most of each and every moment. Some of my happiest moments were spent with her. I could have done with a few less of her attempted match-makings but I know her heart was in a good place. Much like my mom, her heart was as big as they come. Dana sadly lost her battle on November 16, 2015, just a short three years after my mom. I am so grateful that I was able to spend time with her right up until the end. I know for certain that I am a better person for having known Dana.

Oddly enough that was the year my dad was diagnosed with lung cancer. Surreal doesn't even begin to describe going through it again with another parent. You are prepared for the technical stuff but the emotion comes back one-hundred-fold. There are déjà vu moments in doctor's offices and hospital rooms. I am so grateful to my aunt Mary, my mom's sister, for being there for whatever I needed during that time. We tried to find as much happiness during those two years as we could. There were even moments of laughter. It was then that I realized the truth in the statement that if you don't laugh you will cry. So, laugh we did. Knowing what is going to happen really doesn't make it easier. In a way, there were parts of it that seemed worse having already gone through it and knowing what was eventually going to happen. Five years after losing my mom, what seemed completely impossible happened. I lost my dad to cancer on September 29, 2017. My only comfort was knowing he had lived every waking moment wanting to be with my mom again, and he finally was.

It wasn't as easy to pretend I was okay as it was the first time. I wasn't okay. I was literally nothing. I was an empty shell who felt nothing, didn't leave the house unless forced, and lived in the same pair of my dad's pajama bottoms for days on end.

It's a strange feeling to think you are alone in the world. I knew I had family and I had friends but I didn't have my parents and I didn't have the one friend who always understood. I pushed people away. Partly because I didn't want the pity and partly because I didn't want to be around anyone who reminded me of them. I most certainly didn't want to be around anyone who wanted me to be happy.

I put a wall up. If I didn't let anyone get close to me then I couldn't ever have the hurt of losing anyone again. I didn't need anyone. Whether or not that was true, it is what I told myself to get through.

I once again found myself floating in a fog. I tried to remind myself things could be worse, that I was still lucky compared to most, but was I really? How was it fair to have to lose three people who I loved dearly within five years all to the same shitty disease?

But I guess that's the lesson. Life isn't fair. But, fair or not, it keeps going. And I could either spend my time left wallowing in the crappy hand I was dealt or I could take that crappy hand and make something out of it.

I tried therapy for a bit but I don't think I ever found the right fit for me. I slowly found solace on my yoga mat, in being outside, and eventually letting people get close enough to me again. It was hard. I most definitely still kept people at an arm's length, but it was a start.

I had continued walking the Gloria Gemma 5K each year, although it never really felt the same. I was surrounded by people I loved and who cared about me, but it always felt like someone was missing without Dana. The tradition of going to eat afterwards continued and in some small way it helped her to live on with me.

It was a couple of years after losing Dana and my dad that I participated in Gloria Gemma Foundation events that had a bigger impact on me than I could have imagined. In February of 2019, I attended the women's getaway in Sedona. To say the trip was magical would be an understatement. There was an energy that can't be put into words. Being surrounded by so many strong women in such a healing environment is life altering. Yes, there were tears but there was also hope and healing. When you hear the stories of survivors, stories of those still fighting, and stories of those lost, it shifts something inside of you. You begin to realize that there is so much more to living and to love and it doesn't end upon losing someone. In a weird way you start to see it is a beginning; a beginning of you becoming the person that was built from sadness. I knew I would never fully be who I was before all of the loss. But this trip made me start to realize that I could become the best version of me because of the loss. All of the heartache and lessons learned were transformative. I just couldn't see it at the time.

Shortly after, in May of 2019, I participated in the Gloria Gemma Fashion Show. It still shocks me to this day that I did it but something in me knew I had to say yes to the opportunity. Although nervous, I walked down the runway knowing my mom was with me every step of the way. It was also the moment I realized I was allowed to be happy again.

I now fully realized that living was the only way to truly honor the loved ones I lost. Not only did I need to live, but I needed to do it on my terms. I left my job as a kindergarten teacher and pursued a career as a full-time yoga instructor. That eventually turned into me becoming a personal trainer and nutrition coach. I was finally doing what I saw all the women at The Gloria Gemma Foundation all of those years ago doing. I was thriving.

Living is still a work in progress. I still have bad days. I would be lying if I pretended that I didn't cry my eyes out every now and then when a memory hits or a birthday or anniversary comes around. I also thought about quitting and retreating back to solitude, back to the days where I coasted through life going through the motions. But I knew my parents wouldn't want that. Because no matter how hard something was in life, they always encouraged me to see it through. And I certainly can't disappoint them now.

I always question if my parents would be proud of the life I have created. Or what life would be like if they were still here. I often wonder what they would look like now that they'd be older and what their personalities would be like. I worry that a day will come that I don't remember the sound of their voice or that I can't instantly see them when I close my eyes. But I don't know that worrying about those things will change anything.

I know with certainty that I can't waste a minute of however much time I have. I have cultivated a life that I love, surrounded by people I love. I want to travel to all of the places they never got to and do all of the things I wish they could have done.

Would they be proud? I hope so. I think my happiness was all they ever wanted, so I'd like to believe they are happy. I have found my way to a good life.

Would I say grief ever gets easier? Definitely not. But it does get better in time. I don't truly believe that time heals all wounds but it does give us the precious gift too many are denied… time. Time to practice moving through the pain. Time to build strength. Time to find our breath. Time to find moments of happiness. Time to tell our story in the hopes that we can help someone else out there.

The pain of losing my parents and Dana hurts the same today as the day it happened. And although it created a wound that will never fully heal, I have learned to appreciate each moment, to find gratitude for the little things, to take a breath when all seems lost and to live a life that makes me and them proud.

I would never sit here and tell anyone how they should grieve. That is personal to each individual. There is no right or wrong way. There is no good or bad. Are there things that I wish I hadn't done? Maybe. But had that not been my path, I don't know that I would be the same person I am today.

I will tell you that no matter how you get there, life is most certainly worth living. There will be moments to celebrate and you should celebrate loudly. There are good people out there and you need to let them in even if there's a chance of losing them.

You see, I think that's the biggest thing I learned. Grief hurts so much because there was so much love for that person. As much as there is pain in grief, there is also love. And to even have one ounce of that love is worth the pain. It took me a while to actually believe it but the love never ever goes away. There may be moments that you don't feel it but it is there. And I feel it every time I see a butterfly, a sunflower, eat a donut, drink tea, hear Amazing Grace, sit at the beach, among many other things that may seem ordinary to someone else but mean the entire world to me.

Grief will come and go. That is something you need to accept. We cannot control it. Trying to will only frustrate you. So let it come and when it goes keep moving forward. You owe it to yourself and to your loved one. Live a life that makes you proud and that honors all of that love you shared while they were here.

There will be memories and traditions that bring you such comfort. Hold onto those. Embrace them. I love remembering my parents and Dana on their birthdays. I eat or drink something they loved and rest assured I have three of the best angels anyone could ask for in this world. The Gloria Gemma 5k brings me joy as much as it is bittersweet. So, I walk each year for those who can't.

There will also be some memories and traditions that don't bring you comfort. For me, that is where I created new traditions. Christmas was so hard, more than other holidays. Now, I travel on Christmas. I explore somewhere new and make new memories. No matter where I am I can be certain at some point on that trip I see a butterfly.

You will do things that you never dreamt of, like writing this chapter. Trust me there were moments I thought to myself "what were you thinking?" As hard as it was to write, I knew the stories of the people I loved needed to be shared. Maybe more importantly, I realized that I needed people to know there is light and hope through all of the sadness and darkness.

It might sound hard to believe or like a paradox of sorts but the truth is you're never going to get over the loss AND you are also going to be okay. Maybe even more than okay.

As I write this, I am approaching eleven years since I lost my mom. It doesn't seem possible because it seems both like yesterday and a lifetime ago all at once. It also doesn't seem possible that I am here telling you that things will get better. But they do. I am living a life I am proud of, a life that makes me happy. I have learned to appreciate all of the little things that before this I took for granted. In fact, it is the little things like going for a walk with my dog, coffee with a friend, or time alone to recharge that make me the happiest. So, if you ever doubt that things won't ever get better, I can tell you from experience they absolutely do get better. Believe me when I say your life will be beautiful again, just in different ways. You just have to be open to it and of course always be aware of the butterflies.

Patricia & Anthony Pirolli

Dana A. Cardillo

CHAPTER 2

The "C" Word

In Loving Memory of
(Alma) Veronica (Guerra, Berrio, Caicedo, DeLaCruz) Martinez
April 19, 1961 – August 26, 2022

By Jennifer Aracely Berrio Ortiz

In 2009, our world began to change. The "C" word became a common theme. Before this, I never really knew anyone with cancer, not personally, not any of my loved ones. The first person was my dad, Carlos A. Berrio born on December 29, 1955 and passed on September 3, 2010 diagnosed with Stage III Pancreatic Cancer. When he passed at fifty-four years young, I was only thirty-one years old.

In 2011 my mom said, "I think you need to go with me to this doctor's appointment."

The doctor said: Stage I Breast Cancer. Again! The "C" word!! How?! I dropped to the floor. Her doctor asked, "Why is she taking this news so bad?"

My mom held me and said "She just lost her dad."

I felt shattered. How could this be happening? Both my parents were diagnosed within such a short window. My perspective on life began to shift. At this time my son was three years old. He had already lost his grandfather at the age of two. Would he remember either one of them? Would I be an orphan soon? I am learning this is where my grief began. There are many unresolved issues I still haven't faced and I may never receive all the answers to my questions.

Within the same year, my mother-in-law was diagnosed with Stage IV Follicular Lymphoma. By the time I met with her doctors, it was the first time I was asked if I had a medical background. She would beat it, as well as Pancreatic Cancer a few years ago. She is truly a survivor.

Our lives had been consumed with surgeries, chemotherapy, radiation, tests, and follow ups all over Rhode Island and Massachusetts. Both my parents were the first and only to be diagnosed with cancer in their families out of all their siblings. My father was from Colombia, he was one of nine children. My mom was from Guatemala, she was one of six children. She was fifteen years old when she arrived in the United States after a devastating earthquake. She was seventeen years old when I was born and then she had my two brothers in her second marriage. Being left a single mom after two unsuccessful marriages I began to see my mom's strength. I was quite a bit older than the boys, we are nine and eleven years apart.

I got married at sixteen years old because of my need for independence. Basically I just didn't want a curfew. I moved to Pawtucket for a year and a half then moved right back into the family home where I still reside. During that short period was the first time we didn't share the same roof. I would still drive back to Providence every morning to get my brothers ready for school and then go to high school myself. I knew she still needed my help with the boys. My school was a few blocks away. Either way, I had to come to Providence. Why not come and help her. We were always a team after all.

She wanted me to have a baby so bad when I had been with my husband for fifteen years. The agreement was for her to retire from work to be fully available to babysit. She was planning her retirement when I found out I couldn't get pregnant. I had pituitary adenoma, a tumor in my pituitary gland that had my hormones out of whack, making me infertile. So began the journey with infertility treatments. Over a year later, her "King" was on his way. In January 2008 he was born.

On June 29, 2011 my mom had a partial lumpectomy and then six weeks of radiation. We thought it was over. They had caught it early in Stage 1. They spoke so confidently, it sounded like it was quick and easy. She was put on Tamoxifen which caused her to have a metal taste in her mouth. We had six years of joy. After the five-year mark they start to use the word remission. We started to feel safe and secure. Then the rug was pulled out from underneath us again. It was just the tip of the iceberg. If only it could have ended here. Early prevention is key after all, right? How different our lives would have been. I would still have my Mami.

I remember the first time we had to shave her head. The kids were so little. We didn't want them to be scared of her when her hair would eventually fall out. We decided to make it a family event. I made six different ponytail braids around her head. We each took a turn cutting one off, then had fun buzzing the rest off. I wish I had recorded this now. This was before phones were so easily available to record every moment of our lives. It felt good to do it as a family and take a little control back. Our lives were on an emotional rollercoaster.

We had a very open line of communication. My Mom was truly my first best friend. I lived on the second floor and she on the first floor of the house she left my brothers and me. My daily routine would be to pop my head into the first floor before work. If her bedroom door was cracked open, she would be semi-awake. If it was closed, she wasn't awake at all. Unless I had something I needed to tell her, I would just leave to work. We are not morning people. I didn't want to disturb the three layers of sleeping masks, three body pillows, and three heart pillows of her slumber to hear the groan of *what do you want?* I would see her after work. If she wasn't home, we would know of her arrival by the sound of her car alarm. She would joke by saying I'm going to park around the corner so you guys don't know when I'm home. My son would scream "Wela is home!" This I miss the most, seeing her every day.

She held down so many jobs simultaneously and was determined to continue her education. I remember checking her homework. When I was thirty years old, she finally graduated from Providence College with a bachelor of arts in liberal studies. She was so excited for the three-day graduation weekend. She had me attend so much of it with her. On the third day there was a moment she took off her sash and said "I dedicate this to you because I wouldn't have been able to finish without you." I treasure that moment and the sash.

She was fully devoted to being the best Wela in the world. When the kids got older, they began school and needed less of her attention. Over time, she realized she was losing the English language. She discussed this with a dear neighbor of ours that was a college professor. She began to tutor my mom. After her passing and during a heartfelt conversation with our neighbor she told me she had some writing my mom had done during one of their lessons. I was so excited to hear this. I cherish any piece I find of her since her passing. I asked her to send it to me. Here it is:

"My name is Alma Veronica Guerra Lopez, I was born in Guatemala City Guatemala. I am the 5th of 6 children. I was raised by my grandmother (my father's side) and uncles, aunts, older siblings and cousins. A Chilmol of people raise me. From the stories my parents told us, the adventurous one was my mother (my family did have a restaurant, but where not doing to good money wise). My mother was offer a position in Los Angeles to come and clean a house. She went back and forth a few times maybe two or three. My father was told not to let her come back alone, because she was beautiful and young and someone can take her from her. They both decided to come to New York City, where they maybe knew one person. They came with a visa, and while they work they were able to obtain their green card, through and employer. They both work full time and part-time, both learn the train system to move around without speaking any English. They use to share an apartment with maybe with at least 5 more people so they all share the rent and utilities. They just to support themselves while they send money to Guatemala to support all of us completely and save money to start immigration paper work to bring all of us to the land of opportunities. While doing that they started to visit Rhode Island and my father thought it was a better place to raise their children. When they started the paperwork my father was offer to bring all his children at the same time but he got afraid of our upbringing and thought it was better to do two at the time. My four older siblings came first and when it was time for me and my younger brother to come, they already have move to Rhode Island. From my memories I think I was maybe three the first time my mother left and then I was about five when they both left. I remember crying and my older sister carrying me, me given my hands to my mother because I did not want her to leave."

She had overcome so much already from domestic abuse, divorces and child molestation from multiple family members. She would get married four times in total. Each husband got younger and younger. The last one is only twenty-three months older than me. The joke was she would take their youth to keep herself looking so young. Each of my parents were married four times. I wonder if they were both alive if that number would climb? Who would win having the most marriages?

I will be celebrating my thirty-year anniversary with my husband this year. We actually got married on the same day. My first and only, and her third marriage. Not many people knew she was getting married as they showed up and found their seats for my wedding outside. I remember calling for her, yelling her name out the bedroom as I was getting ready. Her cousin told me she's in the other room doing that "thing." With her third husband, she would move to East Providence with the boys. After that divorce, we shared the same roof again up until she passed. I would tell her if she added up all her marriages it probably wouldn't amount to my one.

Coming from my childhood of multiple stepmoms and stepdads, I wanted a different family dynamic for my son. Raising him with his dad in the house has definitely been a different experience. My mom would say that my husband was her eldest child. It was funny when my husband ended up being two years older than her fourth husband.

She was a case manager, social worker, translator, lead inspector, Avon lady, popular club, and community advocate. The last few years, I got more deeply involved in advocacy. Through Covid, I got close with the Lt. Governor at the time. When he became Governor, he named me as a senior advisor on his transition team. This made her scream with pride. She wanted me to send her every article and news video I would partake in. She said, "You have reached the level I always aspired to, I'm so proud of you."

I now serve on many small business and education boards and committees. As I compiled this list, I wondered how I could wear all these hats.

- Governor's Workforce Board (Strategic Investments Committee & Youth Career Pathways Advisory Committee)
- RI Department of Health Hairdressers Board
- Vice-Chair RI Small Business Coalition
- District Wide Advisory Council
- Parent Advisory Council
- Classical Parent Ambassador
- School Improvement Team for Classical

- CHSCA Co-President
- CTE Committee

She would apologize for how she raised me. She thought she was too hard on me in comparison to my brothers. Being the oldest and only girl comes with a lot more responsibility, including cooking and cleaning. I had less privileges, like going to friends' houses or dare I ask for a sleepover. That was barely allowed. The boys had it much easier in my eyes. They still do. I always noticed the difference, but it is what made me a tough cookie. She made me strong. It comes in handy now that she left me the Trustee/Executor of everything. I bear a lot of responsibility. Thank goodness because it's the only thing holding me up now.

In August 2017, it was another diagnosis of the other breast, a totally different type of breast cancer, Stage II. After much testing and second opinions, the decision was made. On October 10, 2017 she underwent a bi-lateral double mastectomy with latissimus muscle flap, with immediate breast reconstruction, and tissue expanders. Some hiccups including four anaphylactic reactions, fever, one ambulance, two emergency rooms, five attempts at an IV, and nitro cream to save the skin that was dying. She pulled through all of that just to be told she had to do four rounds of chemotherapy.

By this time, I had finally convinced her to sign up to be part of the Gloria Gemma Foundation. She had not wanted to sign up the first time she was diagnosed, expressing that she was too young to need such resources. I knew the second diagnosis was going to be rougher. I showed her all the support that she can receive and how they supported the family in general. She finally agreed to let me sign her up. She was part of the metastatic breast cancer group. It was one of the best decisions she could have made not only for her but also for me.

She received her surgery bag which contained her first little heart pillow. When they found out that it was a double mastectomy, they gave her another one. She loved those little heart pillows. They kept her so comfortable after the major surgery. Somehow she ended up with a third mini-pillow. I have now kept these for me. I treasure them, hug them, travel, and sleep with them.

After 2017's double mastectomy, they started monthly food deliveries.

Our entire Thanksgiving meal was catered. We both loved the convenience of that, and we began having some parts of it catered afterwards. That's why I decided for our first Thanksgiving in 2022 without her, we would go to a restaurant. There was no way I could fathom doing it without her.

One of her favorite events was Passport to Survivorship Expo. She would go from table to table gathering all the goodies, especially pens! She would fill up both of our bags, but when we got home she would dig through my bag to see what she wanted to keep. We enjoyed the classes of jewelry making and the sound baths (my favorite).

The 2022 expo was five weeks after she passed. I had to attend. My best friend and son joined me for moral support. I tried to hold it together but when I saw the table representing her hospice, I lost it. Another altering experience I had that day was running into her Oncologist. The Oncologist had given her a clean bill of health November 1, 2021. I reminded him what she always told him "Listen to your patients, we know our body." Being able to have a chat with him brought me closure I never expected to receive.

Onto 2023, to be there with the release of this book will definitely be full circle. It will be shortly after her one-year anniversary of passing. She was a torch bearer in the last Flames of Hope Event in 2019 before the pandemic. I am so HONORED that on the day this book gets released, in the evening event, I will carry a torch in her name.

From the food delivery services monthly, the Thanksgiving meal, the meditation yoga classes, etc… the most touching thing has been the friendships that were created, especially Jane. She got so close to my mom and me. At the end-of-life stages she came and sat next to Mom, looked at me and said to go upstairs shower, eat, rest. I'm here. I felt the complete and utter feeling that I was leaving her with someone so safe, a family member by choice, not by blood. That is the gift she left me by signing up to be part of this community. The Gloria Gemma Foundation has been one of my biggest supporting resources to get through the loss of my mother. I joined two support groups. One in person at their Pawtucket office. Another one on Zoom. That's what led to me being part of this book.

March 17, 2019. Again, CANCER. I was pissed! I looked at the doctor straight in his eyes and said how could she have breast cancer? She has NO BREASTS! It was in the chest bone. Off to Boston we went. Then she had another four relapses, more surgeries, chemotherapy and radiation. Okay done. She had done EVERYTHING. She was a survivor once again. Right?!?!

Covid hit. Not just our world changed but the whole world changed. We felt prepared. We had sanitizer, gloves, and masks in stock. We had been trying to keep her safe all throughout the years. The protocols to come into the house went to another higher level. All five kids were home. We spent so much time enjoying each other. It was a bit of relief from the monotonous life.

As the world slowly opened, I worried about returning to work. One of my brothers never stopped working. He couldn't because one of his jobs is at a hospital. He took extra precautions coming around. We were all so careful because she was high risk. After months of lockdown, she went to lunch with a few close friends. One was asymptomatic. That's all it took for fifteen of us to get Covid. We got through it. She began to feel things, but Covid limited the doctors' visits and testing. She was having breathing issues. They attributed it to her having Covid. Go see your pulmonologist, the oncologist told her.

One test, another test. In January 2022, Stage IV. The cancer was now in the chest bone (again), lungs, hip, liver (seven spots), and the brain. She said I'm done. I don't want to fight anymore. I said okay, what do you want to do? We discussed all options with her doctors. They suggested palliative care. It was clear that this treatment plan was not to cure her. She opted for shots to slow the rate of growth down.

She had gamma knife surgery on March 29, 2022, for the 5ml brain tumor in her parietal lobe because if not she would only have a few weeks left. Then five rounds of radiation on the hip to help with mobility. She didn't want to do much more. Let's enjoy the time we have left. Six months to two years they said. The shock was so huge. I felt I had let her down. Everything I pushed her to do the last time. Was it worth it? Why did the cancer keep coming back? Why my mom? Was it because she was too good? Too good to be on this earth. I knew she was scared. She tried to prepare me for everything possible. She needed to know I could handle things. We met with the lawyer. Got the Will and Trust in order. She made me a huge binder with all her bills, passwords, and important information. It has definitely helped out tremendously.

We discussed ideas and final wishes. She came up with let's drive cross-country. Sixteen days after her brain surgery, we took off. I was so worried,

I discussed the trip in detail with her brain surgeon. He was so understanding and reassuring. He wanted the trip to happen. He said GO, make the memories. I know a doctor in every state. If anything happens, call me and I'll tell you which hospital to bring her to.

April 14-28, 2022, we executed a trip of a lifetime. One 32-foot RV, nine of us, all her kids, all her grandkids, my husband and her cousin Roselia. We visited twenty-five states in two weeks. Major stops were four corners, Grand Canyon, Horseshoe Bend, Las Vegas, Los Angeles, Huntington Beach, Sequoia National Forest, Big Sur, Golden Gate Bridge, San Francisco, Yellowstone, Mt. Rushmore, and Chicago. She was overjoyed. We celebrated her last birthday, on April 19, 2022, as she turned 61. We baked, had a cookout, and decorated the RV. She talked about it with everyone and showed the amazing magical pictures off. I cherish the memories we made on this trip. The unlimited quality time we had together. I loved to see her so happy. She always had a grandchild to snuggle with and spoil.

When we arrived in LA, I realized how unfriendly LA was to RVs. We couldn't find a safe place to park so my husband could sleep for a few hours. My cousin drove us around until we found a safe space. We all ended up getting breakfast at Huntington Beach in the morning. The way my mom poured love onto my cousin's kids reinforced what her obituary said that she was everyone's Wela (Grandma).

A dear friend gave us a game the day we left. It was called "How well do you know your family?" I video recorded so much of it because we all were laughing at the questions and challenges it made us do. For example, it was my brother Jonathan's turn. He had to name one thing in the RV, and we had to hand it to him. First one won. I recorded as we all eagerly awaited his request. He said cookies! Well, I was sitting on the couch and the cookies were stored above my head. The stampede that ensued upon me was hilarious. To see Mami laughing so hard was priceless. I think back now and wish we had taken more time. Maybe an entire month. It's one of those life choices you doubt after the fact. Now she's gone and we can never get more time with her. I am utterly grateful for the time we did have. Even though when we got back, she did say I don't want to see any of you for a year. I gave her two days of space and she called me, why haven't you stopped by the first floor. That was our bond.

In June 2022, I called her to ask a simple question. She was crying. I asked, what's going on? She said nothing. I went straight home. She had a Dana Farber (Donna Farmer as she called it) appointment the next day. She didn't want to go. The shots were causing her a lot of leg pain. We knew it was a side effect. We talked it out and went to Boston. She decided to stop all treatment. The next step was hospice. So began the decline. Home & Hospice was so helpful. All of June, July, and August, the extra help was nice with the CNA, companions, Chaplin, and social worker.

August 3rd was her last appointment, with the results from her last scan. The one she wanted a friend to take her to because she didn't want me missing any more work. I refused. She ended up having a panic attack. They had to come get me to calm her down and sat me on the other side of the door so I could be there in a second if she yelled for me. The spread in the last two months was astronomical. The seven spots on the liver multiplied to over thirty, they stop counting after that many. The doctor said a few weeks to no more than three months. Everyone tried so hard to keep me positive but I'm a realist. I had to get things going, in order. I started taking pictures and videos. I learned from my dad's passing that I needed her voice recorded. We started planning the funeral, the clothes, the flowers, the music, and the eulogy.

August 6th, she stayed home alone while we went to Patriot Place for the day. I came home and her husband was feeding her soup. I looked at her and asked what happened. She was completely out of it. We didn't know she had overdosed on medication. She would confuse the medications, not sure which one was for what. How much to take of each one. She couldn't remember what she had taken or how much of it. I called the hospice hotline number immediately. There wasn't much to be done, just monitor her. My brother Jonathan had come home from work. I texted Oscar, he came over. All four of us somewhat fit in her full-size bed. My son Uriel on the couch next to her bed. The four of us watched her sleep. We made sure she was breathing. A few hours later she woke up, looked at all of us and said why are you all here? I stopped working full time after that. One of the hospice nurses brought me syringes, taught me how to add food coloring to all the liquid meds. It scared me to the point that I would not leave her for more than a few hours after this. No one else was allowed to prepare her medications.

I ordered her a mini fridge to keep on her nightstand, in which only three of each medication would be kept in at any given time. She still wanted some independence. Every dose had to be written in the notebook. I had an intricate system to assure her safety. Only if you went through my training would I feel comfortable leaving someone else in charge and only for a few hours. My Type A personality shined. This way, I could tell what she had taken and how many doses.

By this time, the family began to move in with us. Her siblings were making their way to RI, as well as her mom. Her niece Alyssa flew in and barely left her side. I cleared the living room. I bought a sleeper couch. I added another bed to the spare room. Local family members began taking shifts. The support was tremendous and much appreciated.

I had been through hospice with my grandfather that passed away in our house. My dad passed away at my grandmother's house in Pawtucket. I missed his passing by a few minutes. I didn't want to miss hers. I knew the end was near. She was sleeping a lot. The night she choked on me giving her medications, I knew it was going to be her last night in the house. I wouldn't leave her side anymore. We discussed this. I wanted to be there when she passed. She brought me into this world. I wanted to see her out. I told my son to go upstairs and go to bed. He left, or so I thought. I was quietly crying, knowing how fast things were going downhill. He came back into the room and caught me crying. He wouldn't leave my side now. It was just the three of us that last night, which I am thankful for.

Hospice came about 5am. Not her regular nurse, an on-call one. The nurse said she didn't meet criteria for a transfer. We were taking too good care of her. Rachel, our dear friend, had come over to assist. By this time, she was comatose. The house began to fill up with so many people. I lost count of the thirty to forty family and friends that came in and out. The hospice team showed up with her main nurse, social worker, and chaplain. The nurse looked at her, looked at me and said we need to talk.

We went upstairs to my apartment. She said it's time to move her. I said that I thought she didn't meet the criteria. What about all the family here that wants to keep seeing her? They said that wasn't the plan and you know that. She told us, you told us. You're letting your emotions change things up. I said, but if I move her only four people are allowed in the room. Well, three, because I'm not leaving. She said okay, blame me if you have to but this was the plan and we are sticking to it. I said okay, execute it.

When you're pregnant you pack your hospital bag in advance. Well, I should have done the same for this, hospice bags. What did I need for her? Clothes, pillows, Angels, pictures. I ended up with a whole suitcase that six months later I have yet to unpack.

Then I ran upstairs and threw some clothes and stuff for me in a bag. How long would we/I be there? I forgot the toiletries. Thankfully Home & Hospice had little bags for us. I was relieved because I knew it wasn't just me that wasn't prepared. The ambulance came to transport her. Jonathan and I rode with her. She was put in Room 301. The signs began. Her numbers. We were nine days away from the anniversary of my dad's passing. Were they going to share the date? Moving her was the best decision. She had this peace about her. Like she was sleeping beauty. Jon took the chair. They made up the bed for me. I think I slept maybe a few hours. Her longtime best friend Lana came in the early morning hours. Nurses and CNA's came in to switch her position. Jon and I flipped sides. I had instructions to carry out. Things I had to say, music to play, her mantra. It took me about three hours. I kept in the back of my head a poem that her cousin Lucky shared with me the day before she passed.

Expected Death

When someone dies, the first thing to do is nothing. Don't run out and call the nurse. Don't pick up the phone. Take a deep breath and be present to the magnitude of the moment.

There's a grace to being at the bedside of someone you love as they make their transition out of this world. At the moment they take their last breath, there's an incredible sacredness in the space. The veil between the worlds open.

We're so unprepared and untrained in how to deal with death that sometimes a kind of panic response kicks in. "They're dead!"

We knew they were going to die, so their being dead is not a surprise. It's not a problem to be solved. It's very sad, but it's not cause to panic.

If anything, their death is cause to take a deep breath, to stop, and be really present to what's happening. If you're at home, maybe put on a kettle and make a cup of tea.

Sit at the bedside and just be present to the experience in the room. What's happening for you? What might be happening for them? What other presences are here that might be supporting them on their way? Tune into all the beauty and magic.

Pausing gives your soul a chance to adjust, because no matter how prepared we are, a death is still a shock. If we kick right into "do" mode, and call 911, or call the hospice, we never get a chance to absorb that enormity of the event.

Give yourself 5 minutes or 10 minutes, or 15 minutes just to be. You'll never get that time back again if you don't take it now.

After that, do the smallest thing you can. Call the one person who needs to be called. Engage whatever system needs to be engaged, but engage them at the very most minimal level. Move really, really, really, slowly because this is a period where it's easy for body and soul to get separated.

Our bodies can gallop forwards, but sometimes our souls haven't caught up. If you have an opportunity to be quiet and be present, take it. Accept and acclimatize and adjust to what's happening, Then, as the train starts rolling, and all the things that happen after a death kick in, you'll be better prepared.

You won't get a chance to catch your breath later on. You need to do it now.

Being present in the moment after death is an incredible gift to yourself, it's a gift to the people you're with, and it's a gift to the person who's just died. They're just a hair's breath away. They're just starting their new journey in the world without a body. If you keep a calm space around their body, and in the room, they're launched in a more beautiful way. It's a service to both sides of the veil.

Credit for the beautiful words——Sara Kerr, Ritual Healing Practitioner and Death Doula, Death Doula beautiful art by Columbus Community Deathcare.

I held her with both hands. I watched her breathing change. I saw her last breath. I felt her last heartbeat. I just held her for ten minutes. Just her and I. It was a magical transitional moment. Jon woke up, looked at me and knew. I said yes, she's gone. He said, "What do we do?" I said nothing.

Hold our mother. It was just the three of us for another twenty minutes. It was such a gift. 8:33 am, she left us. She broke my heart. Oscar showed up shortly after 9:00 am, Jon had texted him that our mom had passed. We pressed the nurse's button. She came and did her tests. She said, "Sorry, she's gone, do you need time?" I said, "oh no we had our time, get her ready for visitors please."

They gave me a private room to begin the calls. I called my husband and son first. It was high school orientation day. He had to be there by 1:00pm. He had to come see her before that. Who was next? Her mom? Siblings? I remembered I had her phone (still do). They have a group chat and talked all the time. I rang the group. Telling my grandmother that her daughter had died wasn't easy or my aunts, their baby sister, my uncle, his baby sister, my uncle Kiko, his older sister, best friend, confidant. Slowly, they made their way over to see her body. Several other family members and friends came by. After all the visits, the nurse called the funeral home. My husband and I walked her out to the hearse. We then went to join our son. As she wanted, life must go on.

My brothers and I went to meet with the funeral home. She had planned it all out. She made it so simple. The day of the wake, she began texting me (sort of) messages saying "miss you". Her phone would get notifications that were significant in signs, her numbers. I went to shower, as I remember it was a hot day. I was thinking that I'm not going to do my hair or makeup. I heard her say "you are my queen, look like it!" I had done her hair and make up the day before. I decided I would do my makeup exactly the same. This gave me strength. Don't cry. Don't mess up your makeup. We welcomed over 250 guests at her wake. People we hadn't seen in years came from her spiritual groups. Family traveled from Florida, Texas, and Guatemala. The Governor and the Lt. Governor came. We received citations from the Speaker of the House, Congressman Langevin, and Providence City Council.

At her wake, we were each handed handwritten letters she left us. This showed me how scared she was to leave us. I've never thought much how she must have felt all the years she battled. She battled to give us more time with her. I can now begin to imagine and comprehend that fear. As a mother myself, the fear of leaving my son behind. Have I taught him enough? Does he know how much I love him? Will I leave him enough memories of me?

I understand why my mom needed to hear from me. I will be okay. Lies, it was all lies. I am not okay. I still needed her! She was one of the few people on this earth that fully understood me. In the letter she wrote to Oscar she left this line: "I do wish you can work together with your sister. Please be patient with her. You know she can be a bitch but she loves you and will defend you." I am so proud to say that the three of us have grown much closer together since losing her. She would be so happy.

The cremation was private. I knew I wasn't going to be able to hold it together as I did at the wake. We all pushed her casket into the incinerator, I pushed the button that would take my Ma's human body away from me forever. The ashes were ready the next day. I had already planned to return to work. I picked her up and off to work we went. I brought her home that afternoon and put her box in her room. Her mother and siblings were able to spend some time with her before they flew home. She had passed eight days apart from my dad.

Her cousin helped me plan the spreading of her ashes ceremony. She wanted open water. My cousin picked the perfect coordinates. Her birth date was in them. I needed a numeric symbolism behind it. He also shared a birthday with my mom, so it was special in different ways. We needed two boats as there were seventeen people. It was an early, beautiful, and majestic morning. It was my dad's twelfth death anniversary. Her fourth husband carried the ashes in the car to the marina. We brought some of the flowers from the wake. We put on her music and mantra. We threw the flowers into the water. I could see all the lobster traps. She loved lobster. We each grabbed a handful of ashes and spread them. With what was left of the ashes, I sat on the edge of the boat with her Princess, my eight-year-old niece, Aadyn. I taught her how to make a heart with Wela's ashes. When we were done, we jumped in. One last swim with her. It was September third, the water was so warm. One of the sayings that has meant a lot to me is "Great grief only comes out of Great Love."

She left us. Me, her Queen. My brothers, Oscar Javier, and Jonathan Ariel. Her King, my son, Uriel. The other Queen, her first grandchild, A'Lijah. The Princess, Aadyn. My husband, her Babes, Robert. Her husband, Luis. A month after she passed my nephew was born, oh how she would have adored him. He knows it also. He throws himself to the box her ashes came in and to her pictures. It's like he knows that's my Wela. I play him videos of her. I want him to hear her singing and laughing. I will make sure he knows all about her.

We are all forever changed. Still trying to figure out our lives without her. She was our glue. The way she loved us was indescribable and unconditional. We have been cheated out of more years with her. Her presence is forever around. I see the signs. She knew my real heart.

Losing my Mami has changed me in so many ways. Working through my grief is a daily task. Writing this chapter has been healing on many different levels. It has propelled the grieving process tremendously. There are things I hadn't dealt with when I lost my father. Experiencing the drastic grief from losing one parent to losing both. The emptiness of feeling like an orphan even at the age of forty-three.

The relationships I've lost from family and friends have been life changing. Some were near and dear to my heart. Some I wanna scream Mira! I miss you! Some I say good riddance. The betrayal is beyond hurtful. Some seem to not even grieve for her. For months I've had the mindset of what would my mom do in a certain situation. That only led to people taking advantage of me and abusing my grief. I am now in the next chapter of grief. Figuring out who I am now without my mother. My voice of reason is gone. I'm in this ocean learning how to swim all over again. Floating in this abyss. She was my buoy.

I've had this notion that I need to get through the first year. First of every occasion without her, birthdays, holidays, and milestones. Each of them has been difficult in their own way. What has worked for me is pre-planning. It helps me to at least know what I will be physically doing that day because emotionally I won't be controllable. We traveled for Christmas, New Years, and the hardest was my birthday. Having a birthday without the person that brought you into the world is excruciating and painful.

What would have been her sixty-second birthday was also quite the challenge. We all got together and had one of her favorite meals and her favorite red-velvet cake. We sang her Happy Birthday. That was weird but felt proper. Were we supposed to? Who knows. There's no rules on what is the proper thing to do. I make it up as I go. I let my gut and my heart guide me.

Since beginning this journey of writing this book I've had my first

Mother's Day without a mother. Another hard pill to swallow. The plan was to attend a proper English tea party with my cousin visiting from out of state, her daughters, and my best friend. After that, I just floated through the day. I awaited all the signs I knew she would send me and boy did she ever.

I had picked up my nieces from the hotel and was bringing them home to spend the afternoon together. As I turned onto my street, I saw the corner store was open. My nieces love this stuff. I had taken them to a thrift store the day before and one was looking for vinyl. They sell vinyl, CD's, DVD's, cassettes, and more. I found a cassette that my Ma had gifted me for Christmas, 1990. The same singer we had seen live in concert the night before, Vanilla Ice. As I began to cry, my niece consoled me. The older niece came over and said I'm buying it for you! I asked the girls if I could go wait for them at my neighbor's house where I had parked a few steps away. I was feeling overwhelmed. I made my way over and my neighbor had left, but I went to her backyard and sat down. She has this serene adorable little garden yard. There's a bunch of wind chimes around. As I sat there crying the wind chimes began making noise. Not as if wind was going through them, as if someone was flicking them with their finger. I took out my phone to record, but they stopped. I stopped recording, they started again. I hit record, and they stopped again. I said Ma, I want to record it. They started to play again and continued as I recorded.

We went home. My brother asked me for a ride to work, which is rare nowadays. On the way back home, driving behind me was a dear family member that made us beautiful candles in remembrance of her. Having three full red-lights to chat with her and her sister seemed a bit surreal, especially in Downtown Providence. No cars around beeping to make us move forward. It's like the Universe, or Ma, was making special time for us to chat.

I got back home to five kids hanging out. We climbed into bed and picked a movie. Well, my niece picked "Where the Crawdads Sing." I would have never picked this movie out on my own. Another moment that was meant to be. In the movie there is a scene where her mom is waiting for her at the end of her life. I lost it! Crying my eyes out. I said I want that! I want my Mami waiting for me! My niece felt so bad that she had picked this movie. As she hugged me apologizing, I said no baby, it was the perfect movie! I know my Ma will be waiting for me, this just proved that.

There were so many more signs and moments that I felt her presence some days stronger than others. This helps my grief tremendously.

She had this aura about her that's hard to describe. The way she unconditionally loved me and everyone. She forgave easily. She was always in a happy mood when she greeted you. No matter what she was going through or how much pain she was in. Always wanting to help others. She always had time for you. She loved Reiki, stones, Angels, trinkets, coffee, seafood, and massages. I asked family and close friends to say some words about her. I chose to share my book with them to give the reader a broader spectrum of who my mother was. Here is what I received from others:

Her son, Oscar Javier Caicedo

Oh my sweet, sweet mother, a heart of gold she had. I have to blame her for giving me the same heart. The heart to always help others before me. My mother was well loved and respected throughout the community, even the support from our city and state leaders. From helping campaigns to helping immigrants get their citizenship. I always said if it wasn't for my mother's illness, she would be Mayor of Providence one day. My mother learned quickly coming to this country and graduated with her bachelor's from PC.

For everlasting memories I have of you. How each time you needed your favorite drink "sex on the beach," your wine, or an ice-cold Corona. Memories from childhood to adulthood. I know I was a troubled young teen, my run-in with the law, and becoming such a young father. But you always stuck by me as much as I scared you in my teen years. My biggest regret was being that distant son, the always-working son. Yes I've made my life for the better. And I thank my mother for never giving up. But there's things I can't get back. What money can't buy, and that's my mother's love.

What I hold dearest from my adult memories with her. One week before she died, it was a Saturday, and she was so alert, sitting up straight and talking but you could tell her body and mind wasn't one hundred percent. I knew then to have our deepest conversations. There's promises I made to her in our talk that I will fulfill. In our talk, we discussed relationships, being alone, work, goals, self-healing, and more. We shared the biggest hug. In that hug I knew that time was coming to an end as she felt so fragile. I held everything in me not to break down. Almost like I wanted to be strong for her to know that I'll be okay. I was happy she got to react to my good news of myself having an offer accepted on an investment property and having a closing date. I remember telling her I want to take a photo with you in front of the house, Ma. I told you I'll get it done, Ma, I always accomplish my goals. Her response: I knew you could do it, Papi, you are so hardworking and driven. Followed by yes, Papi, if I have enough strength I would like to go see the house. But I knew, I knew as I had watery eyes. My mother wasn't making it to the closing date. Right after our big hug, I said I want to take a video for my unborn son. I want to say a special message to him. As I get my phone ready, I turn my video on. Her first words:

"Hellooooo, my baby boy. Brah!" I immediately started to tear up. When she saw my tear, she then started tearing up during her message to her unborn grandkids. She knew, I'm not gonna have the chance to meet you. It literally broke my heart. My son was born one month later. I hold this special message video dearly. I can't wait to show my son. This is your Wela.

I love you Ma and I'm going to continue to accomplish the goals we spoke about. I will continue to make you proud.

Her son, Jonathan Ariel Caicedo

Dear Ma, when I was born you said I took your heart. When I was young I didn't understand, but I do now as an adult. I inherited your compassion and the want for good deeds. I love you, Ma.

Her granddaughter, A'lijah Imani Maree Caicedo Maddox

My Abuela was very well known, and she knew and loved everyone in her life. No matter how upset she was, she never got violent or loud. She was gentle and soft-spoken. I remember when we found a stray cat in the driveway and she felt so bad for him that she went inside and got him a raw hotdog to eat. Soon after, she got him his shots at the vet and we named him Oreo, and claimed him as our cat for two years. She was thoughtful and generous. Together, we would sit in bed and eat our favorite nime chow from Apsara. It was our favorite part of our meal. She showed love in so many different ways. It didn't matter where or when but if you laid your head on her lap she would start playing with your hair, and it would put me to sleep a lot.

I remember the day she told me she got cancer again; she picked me up from my house and said, "Did Mommy tell you what's wrong with me?" and I said "No? What's wrong…?" she said "The cancer is back." I was a little shocked because to me it felt like she just got recovered from it, but I wasn't worried or scared as I thought "She's gonna beat it again, why wouldn't she? She has so many times, she knows what will help. What will change?" She was always moving, cleaning, cooking, driving, and helping others. She seemed so happy and okay, I would sometimes forget she was sick. It wasn't until we were in Nevada on our road trip for her birthday that I realized she was actually sick. Once my family started taking more photos and more people were coming to visit her and our family from all over the country and more started to come to see her is when it hit a little harder but I honestly didn't think about it that much. I was still in denial. It was the day she started to need help with basic everyday things is when I got scared because I had never seen her like that before.

The day she died, I got a moment alone with her and I just gave her a hug and held her hand until I had to leave. She was like my second mother. I am beyond grateful for everything she has done for me and how much love she has shown me over the past fifteen years. Te Amo.

Her grandson, Uriel Gianni Raul Ortiz (The King)

She was always there, always there with a smile. Maybe not always on time but that's not what mattered cause she made sure you were taken care of. We have to learn to adapt without her but that's okay because we will never forget her, for the mark she has left on our lives is too great to ever forget. As everyone says she was everyone's superwoman, everyone's Wela and that's so true. Wela showed me what it's really like to be strong in life, to do it for the people you love and for the people you hate. To prove yourself against all odds. You are my inspiration. Te amo, Wela.

Her granddaughter, Aadyn Cheyenne Caicedo Maddox (The Princess)

Wela, I love you to the moon and back. I know you were there for my hard times when I would get bullied or hurt. You were the prettiest person I knew. You were also the best cook in the world. I'm glad I got to spend eight years with you. I love you. —*Aadyn*

Her grandson, Jay'vier Amari Caicedo (Written by his father)
Dear Wela,

I didn't get to experience your love or be spoiled in a physical form but I know you are one of my guardian angels who will always watch over me. —Jay'vier

Her sister, Olga Depaz
To my dear sister:

Alma Veronica, it's so hard to write to you knowing I won't see you again in this life! It will be when it is my turn to follow you. It was so beautiful to see you grow up into the strong woman you became. You had a very tough life, so many tears you had to shed because of the troubles life threw at you. But you overcame each one, always trusting God. He knew you had the strength, because if it was me, I wouldn't have been able to endure like you. Regardless of the troubles, you lived a beautiful life. Making so many wonderful memories for us, I wish I had your zest for life. You enjoyed dancing every chance you got. I can still see you, smiling and laughing, with your cute dimple!

Your children, your Queen Jenn, Oscar, and Johnathan, were always your pride and joy. That was probably the toughest thought when you knew it was time to leave. Not to mention your precious grandchildren. I cry just thinking about them.

I wish I had done more for you; I tried my best to console you every time you had trouble and pray and pray for God to comfort you.

Now I just feel loneliness, not being able to talk to you, and confide in someone when I'm having problems. It is just not the same without you. Our brothers and sisters feel the same way, we lost a link, our hearts keep longing for your presence. I prefer to think you took a long trip and will be back soon! Te amo, hermana!

Her brother, Erick Guerra

I miss you! It's hard to find the words to say. I think of you day and night. Although time has eased my pain. I feel I lost part of my heart when you left. I thank God for the years we had together and like we use to talk. Until we see each other again, my sister.

Her niece, Alyssa Crum

In a world full of love, yet never truly taught how.

In a world of constant loss and never taught how to truly let go.

In a world of giving, yet never taught to receive.

A world spent full of doing but no one prepares you for the grief of feeling that you did not do enough

For the Lord feels our suffering and knows our pain, and how we long to see the ones we love up above.

For there will be a day that comes that you will see him or her, ever so slightly familiar in appearance. You will find yourself refusing to look away at that person.

Refusing to let go of this marvelous view God has granted you.

He will remind us of the warmth that we felt while our beloved was still on earth

For their love was our gain how could it slip away so easily into pain

God said "perfect my love and you will let go."

For when a flower blossoms, one sheds its last petal, and it will blow in the breeze till the wind decides it must dance no more.

As for my mourning, I put you to rest my Tia Veronica I will never forget her dance, nor forget her name.

I will love as she loved me.

In God's name, let the breeze take thee.

"For we believe that Jesus died and rose again, and so we believe that God will bring with Jesus those who have fallen asleep in him."
                                        1 Thessalonians 4:13

Her niece, Kylie Crum

The news of her slowly yet rapidly passing hit me like a ton of bricks. I found myself struggling to come to terms with the fact that she was no longer physically with us.

I remember how much she loved getting my massages and how much relief it brought her from her chronic pain. I felt strong, knowing that I had a healer's hand. Giving her massages was something I enjoyed doing, and it gave me comfort knowing that I could alleviate her pain in the slightest ways.

Since her passing, I've found solace in nature walks. It's during these walks that I feel her presence most profoundly. I see her in the vibrant colors of the flowers, in the rustling of the leaves, and in the gentle breeze that surrounds me. When I look outside on rainy days, I could see her dancing and jumping on puddles. I know that she's with me, and that brings me some measure of peace.

Her passing was my first experience with the loss of a close family member at the age of nineteen and it's been a confused emotional journey. I hold onto her items, treasuring them as physical reminders of her life and the love that she shared with us. I protect them with my energy, as if they're a precious part of her that I can keep close to me. Even though she's no longer physically here with us, her spirit lives on in the memories. The love that we share for her is dearly physical to me.

To Titi Veronica, I love you and I'll see you in the rain again.

Her former brother-In-law, Fernando Berrio
3-16-2023

Today is a very special day to write about a wonderful chapter in my life, a special day because it's my birthday. I am feeling blessed having been able to enjoy many celebrations and festivities in my short life. Our friendship began at the beginning of the 80's when I first met you, Veronica. As years went by, our friendship grew and flourished, not realizing it would last forever. One of my most precious weeks we spent together was when Jennifer was born. I used to come over to the house and play with her. Baby her, feed her and Yes! change her stinky, smelly diapers. I would hold her in my arms and nap together on the couch. On occasions we walked to the park, by the river and around downtown Providence. Sometimes we just stayed home listening to music, watching TV, drinking, laughing, partying with my brother and friends. Unfortunately for various situations our lives drifted apart. I started traveling, meeting friends, girlfriends and eventually my first beautiful wife Monica.

As the years went by, I used to visit the family for Thanksgiving, Christmas, summer vacations and special occasions. We would meet for lunch or sometimes, brunch and talk for hours. We have so many good memories but there was one unpleasant moment. I remember the day I told you I was moving to New Jersey you held my hand and gave me a big hug, cried and asked me not to forget about you. We cried, said our goodbyes, and I answered, I will never forget you, I will keep in touch because you are my crying shoulder and advisor for the difficult moments I was going through in my crazy teenage years. I got into the Greyhound bus, waved goodbye and never came back to live in Rhode Island. Imagine this, I remembered working in the diner, saving all my quarters, walking to the nearest payphone, calling you, letting you know how much I missed you, listening to the baby playing around you, telling me all your problems. Me telling you my adventures and before you know it, it ran out of quarters and listening to the phone tone hanging up on us without saying goodbye.

Another funny occasion when we met for lunch, you told me that your marriage was on the rocks and you were thinking of leaving him. Before we knew it, in the middle of our lunch, He walks in. Apparently you hadn't told him we were meeting.

He thought you were having an affair, and when he saw me he cracked up and said it's you! We laughed, he said bon appétit, and left us alone. I am so blessed to have so many wonderful memories with you, even through all our trials and tribulations, marriages and relationships. We kept a strong friendship together. Nothing broke us up, not even the "cancer" could stop the love we had. I enjoyed every moment we spent together.

Your heart of gold is unique, amazing, and very special! I thank God you are part of my life. I thank God for our beautiful families. I have you deep, deep inside my heart and soul. Sometimes I close my eyes thinking about you and dream of the day when I get to hold you, hug you one more time. God is good, life is wonderful and full of happiness. I love you my dear friend, I will see you in heaven or I might see you later!

Her former daughter-in-law, Genesis Maddox Caicedo

My mother-in-law, Veronica, was a one-of-a-kind woman. And while that sounds like a cliche, and I may also be biased, she truly touched everyone she came in contact with. She had a genuine soul and did everything with great intentions and a full heart. I thank her daily for the positive impact she had on my children's lives as well as my own. We lost her entirely too soon, but I am so very grateful for the time we had with her. I love you to the moon and back, Mami!

Her friend, Maria y Felipe Hernandez

Siempre estuvimos la una para la otra, esa llamada, esa visita, ocasiones especiales, la extraño muchísimo. ¿Esa llamada "Como estas Mamita?" Era una persona incondicional en todos los sentidos. Era para mí una hermana. Quería a mis hijos como sus sobrinos de sangre.

Translation:

We were always there for each other, that phone call, that visit, or special occasions, I miss her so much. That phone call "How are you, Mamita?" She was an unconditional person in every way. She was a sister to me. She loved my kids as if they were her blood nephews.

Her friend, Esperanza Vallejo

Es un gran placer tener la oportunidad de compartir un poquito de lo mucho que significo nuestra querida Vero en nuestras vidas.

Veronica fue un ser humano muy noble de un gran corazón, que sacrificaba todo para poder servir a los demás. Siempre se dió con mucha grandeza para todo aquel que le solicito alguna ayuda. Nunca decía no cuando alguien le pedía un favor, lo hacía con alegría sin importar el favor que fuera ni la distancia que tuviera que ir con esa persona.

Tuve la dicha de estar con ella en las buenas y sus momentos difíciles pues me tenía mucho cariño y respeto y siempre que necesita terapias me llamaba como siempre solía decirme "mi señora". Puedo decir que Vero fué una gran luchadora, lucho hasta su último momento. Recuerdo que tres meses antes de su partida me llamo para que fuera a darle Reiki y dos semanas antes todavía me llamaba para que le cambiara la receta de los jugos. Todo esto es una muestra que ella lucho hasta el final de sus días por su salud.

Fue miembro de nuestra Escuela Espiritual ADEUSA por más 12 años, en la cual siempre se entregó al servicio de voluntariado con amor. Tuvo la oportunidad de trabajar como secretaria y tesorera en más de una ocasión y siempre hacia todo lo posible de apoyar el crecimiento de nuestra Escuela Espiritual.

Ella tenía una hermosa conexión con el señor Efraín Villegas Quintero (Maestro DESOTO) el cual fue el fundador de nuestra Escuela Espiritual en más de 15 países del mundo.

Vero con frecuencia expresaba lo agradecida que se sentía por todo el crecimiento espiritual que había adquirido en ADEUSA y como su vida le había cambiado para bien.

Fue una amiga incondicional para todos los que le conocimos en ADEUSA.

Vero gracias por todos los momentos que compartimos juntas, gracias por ser una gran amiga, gracias por darte con tanta grandeza. Tus hermanos de ADEUSA siempre te llevaremos en nuestros corazones.

CON CARIÑO DE TU HERMANA ESPERANZA VALLEJO.

Translation:

It is an immense pleasure to have the opportunity to share a little of how much our beloved Vero meant in our lives. Veronica was a very noble human being with a big heart, who sacrificed everything in order to serve others. She always gave herself with great love to anyone who asked her for help. She never said no when someone asked her for a favor, she did it with joy no matter what favor it was or how far she had to go with that person.

I had the joy of being with her in good times and her difficult moments because she had a lot of love and respect for me, and whenever she needed therapy she called me. She always used to call me "my lady". I can say that Vero was a great fighter. She fought until her last moment. I remember that three months before her departure, she called me to go and give Reiki. Two weeks before, she still called me to change the juice recipe. All this is a sign that she fought until the end of her days for her health.

She was a member of our Spiritual School (ADEUSA) for more than twelve years, in which she always gave herself to volunteer service with love.

She had the opportunity to work as a secretary and treasurer on more than one occasion and always did her best to support the growth of our Spiritual School. She had a beautiful connection with Mr. Efraín Villegas Quintero (Master DESOTO) who was the founder of our Spiritual Schools in more than fifteen countries of the world.

Vero often expressed how grateful she was for all the spiritual growth she had acquired at ADEUSA and how her life had changed for the better.

She was an unconditional friend to all of us who knew her at ADEUSA.

Vero, thank you for all the moments we shared together, thank you for being a great friend, thank you for giving yourself with such greatness. Your brothers and sisters at ADEUSA will always carry you in our hearts.

Her friend, Jenny Dbrasco
CARTA A MI AMIGA

Mi querida Vero, desde que te conocí en el 2014 supe que íbamos a ser muy buenas amigas Cuantas historias compartidas, cuanto nos reímos. Fuimos amigas, hermanas y confidentes.

Durante nuestras convivencias comencé a observar el gran ser humano que eras, siempre preocupada por el bienestar de las personas indefensas como las personas indocumentadas con alguna enfermedad, recuerdo como abogabas con tanto entusiasmo por el bienestar de esas personas un que no las conocieras.

Recuerdo el día que mi doctora de cabecera me dijo que tenía un alto porcentaje de que podría tener cáncer en las tiroides, me acuerdo de que nos fuimos juntas a Boston para hacerme los analices y me sentí muy afortunada de tener una amiga de verdad. Te agradezco tanto el apoyo incondicional en ese momento de incertidumbre donde más se necesita un apoyo emocional. Gracias por hacer ese viaje una aventura, nos reímos de todo lo raro que veíamos, nos fuimos windows shopping y al final un rico almuerzo antes de tomar el autobús para Providence.

En muchas ocasiones veía como dejabas de hacer tus propias cosas personales para ayudar a los demás. Y en muchas ocasiones veía que el dejar a un lado tus responsabilidades provocabas situaciones personales con tu pareja y de igual forma ayudabas aun sabiendo lo que ibas a enfrentar.

Como madre ni se diga, fuiste dedicada con cada uno de tus hijos Fuiste una madre trabajadora incansable, fuiste la abuela más dadivosa y cariñosa que he conocido. Me encantaba como jugabas con tus nietos y de todas las fiestas de sus cumpleaños que con tanto amor ayudabas a organizar.

Mi vero como siempre te llame y te seguiré llamando, quiero que sepas que te admire por tu carácter fuerte y tu mentalidad positiva. Extraño tu amistad incondicional y tu sonrisa franca que te caracteriza aun en los momentos más difíciles. Se que te volveré a ver en cuanto mi alma parta y espero verte para que continuemos riéndonos y contándonos nuestras experiencias.

¡Hasta siempre mi Vero querida!

Translation:
A LETTER TO MY FRIEND

My dear Vero, since I met you in 2014 I knew that we were going to be incredibly good friends. We shared so many stories and we laughed so much. We were friends, sisters, and confidants.

During our time together I quickly observed that you were a great human, always concerned about the welfare of defenseless people like the sick, undocumented people. I remember how you advocated with such enthusiasm for the welfare of the people that you didn't even know.

I remember the day my family doctor told me I had a high percentage that I might have thyroid cancer. I remember we went to Boston together for tests and I felt very lucky to have a real friend. I thank you so much for your unconditional support in that time of uncertainty where emotional support is most needed. Thank you for making that trip an adventure. We laughed at everything strange we saw, we went windows shopping and at the end we had a delicious lunch before taking the bus to Providence.

On many occasions, I witnessed how you stopped doing your own personal things to help others. Also, on many occasions I have seen that putting aside your own responsibilities would cause personal situations with your partner, and you still helped others knowing what you were facing ahead. As a mother, you were dedicated to each of your children. You were a tireless working mother, you were the most giving and loving grandmother I have ever known. I loved to see how you played with your grandchildren and all the birthday parties that, with so much love, you helped organize.

My Vero, as I always call you and I will continue to call you; I want you to know that I admired you for your strong character and positive mentality. I miss your unconditional friendship and your frank smile that characterized you even in the most challenging times. I know that I will see you again as soon as my soul departs, and I hope that we continue laughing and sharing each other's experiences. See you forever, my dear Vero!

Her friend, Magaly

Mi amada Veronica para mí fuiste el angelito que Dios puso en mi vida y en la vida de tantos seres a los cuales nos ayudaba con sus acciones y su solidaridad y le doy tantas gracias a Dios de haberme dado la oportunidad de compartir tantas cosas con ella y a ustedes como familia por haberme permitirme con ella sus últimas horas pues tuvimos la oportunidad de su viaje hacia el mundo Astral pues ella tenía conciencia su nuevo estado de conciencia y que hermoso fueron esas ultimas horas pues me expreso alegría no tristeza y fue un espacio mágico y yo sé que desde el punto de luz donde su Espíritu este nos está bendiciendo en este mundo de las formas. Te amo hija de mi más amado Ángel

Translation:

My beloved Veronica, for me was the little angel that God put in my life and in the lives of so many humans to whom she helped. With her actions and her solidarity, I thank God so much for having given me the opportunity to share so many things with her and as a family for allowing me within her last hours, because we had the opportunity of her trip to the Astral world because she was aware of her new state of consciousness. How beautiful those last hours were because she expressed joy, not sadness, and a magical space. I know that from the point of light where her Spirit is, she is blessing us in this world in so many ways. I love you, daughter of my most beloved Angel.

Her friends, Susana and Leo Bonilla

It is hard to heal our heart when a beloved friend leaves us. I am talking about Veronica, who was not only a friend, but also a confidant, a family member, and a beautiful companion to have around.

Sometimes we do not think that she is not physically with us any longer, because we have not gotten used to that yet; she is always present in our minds, just as if she was still around.

We miss her; we miss her laughter, her compassion, and her love for lobsters.

It will not be possible to replace her, even as time goes by. Our love and gratitude for everything she was will always be there.

Her friend, Betzy Perez

Mom was a force to be reckoned with, and she was also a beacon of light that many people flocked to for help.

Her friend, Marta Reyes

Veronica: la conocí en 1996. Haberla conocido fue como una bendición. Aprendí mucho de ella. Era un gran ser humano. Siempre estaba pendiente de su familia. Trabajaba mucho porque quería que nunca le faltará nada a sus hijos y a sus padres. Como hermana era muy preocupona y como amiga muy leal colaboraba mucho en su comunidad participaba en todo lo que podía, ayudaba a todas las personas que se lo pedía raramente decía no y eso sucedió hasta los últimos días que estuvo acá con nosotros. No sé de dónde sacaba las fuerzas para llevar a otras personas a sus citas médicas. Las personas que tuvimos la dicha de conocerla podemos pensar que así hay gente buena que ayuda desinteresadamente. Ella por sus padres trato siempre de estar al 100. Puedo decir que hizo más de lo que cualquiera se pudo imaginar en este mundo. Luchó como una guerrera contra la enfermedad. Pero algo que le admiré hasta en su lucha de muerte recibió la decisión de Papá Dios con humildad y serenidad. Porque si alguien sabía el significado de la muerte era ella y eso lo aprendí de ella. Todos nos tenemos que ir unos antes que otros, pero todos sí o sí tenemos que tomar el pasaporte para que nos sellen de visado y tomar el viaje eterno. Le encantaba unir a la familia en tiempos festivos, en tiempos de enfermedad ella era la primera en comunicarlo y estaba allí para lo que se ofrecía. Tenía familia grande pero aun así llegó adoptar muchos sobrinos la llamaban Tía y me da el gusto y el orgullo que recibió a mi hija como su nieta adoptiva. Nadie es perfecto tenía sus cosas negativas como cualquiera ser humano. Pero me atrevo a decir que si me piden que ponga en una balanza sus defectos y sus virtudes a mi parecer pesaban más sus virtudes, aunque ella nunca se jactaba de lo que hacía. Los que tuvimos el privilegio de conocerla sabemos que en años habrá otro que mi Vero que Dios la tenga en su Gloria.

Translation:

Veronica: I met her in 1996. To have known her was like a blessing. I learned a lot from her. She was a great human being. She was always looking out for her family. She worked hard because she wanted her children and parents to never lack anything. As a sister she was very concerned, and as a very loyal friend she collaborated a lot in her community. She participated in everything she could, she helped all the people who asked. She her rarely said no and that happened until the last days she was here with us. I don't know where she got the strength to take other people to get to their doctor's appointments. People who had the joy of knowing her can think that there are good people who help selflessly. She always gave herself for her parents 100%. I can say that she did more than anyone could imagine in this world. She fought as a warrior against the disease. But something I admired even in her death struggle is that she received the decision of Papa God with humility and serenity. Because if anyone knew the meaning of death, it was her, and I learned that from her. We all have to leave, some before others, but we all have to take the passport to get a visa stamp and take the eternal journey. She loved to bring the family together in festive times. In times of illness, she was the first to communicate it and was there for what was offered. She had a large family, but still she adopted many nephews and nieces to call her aunt and it gives me the pleasure and pride that she received my daughter as her adopted granddaughter. No one is perfect, she had her negative things like any human being. But I dare say that if I was asked to put her defects and her virtues in a balance, in my opinion her virtues weighed more, although she never boasted of what she did. Those of us who had the privilege of knowing her know that in years there will not be another like my Vero, and that God has her in His Glory.

Her friend, Delia Rodriguez-Masjoan

Te conocí como nos conocíamos en aquel entonces… Madres, Latinas, guerreras, sedientas por ayudar a nuestra gente en la comunidad. Queríamos que nuestra gente progresara, y lo demostramos con ejemplos propios. Estudiamos y nos graduamos de la universidad, para que otras madres Latinas vieran que si se podía lograr. Dejamos relaciones familiares o de amistad, si había abuso, maltrato o discriminación, y apoyamos a mujeres víctimas de violencia doméstica. No teníamos teléfonos, ni computadoras, ni correo electrónico ni redes sociales…. ¡Nuestra red de conexión era pasión, lucha y vida! Eso nos unía como cordón umbilical. Para mantener nuestra salud mental, nos reuníamos cada tanto mes, solo porque sí, a tomar un café, a desayunar, o un traguito… No necesitábamos razón para vernos, y cada encuentro nos alimentaba más el alma para seguir ayudando a nuestra gente. Había un intercambio de admiración la una para la otra, y nuestras historias se entrelazaban con nuestro trabajo comunitario. Ella, mi hermana, mi compañera de lucha, mi Verónica…. No necesitaba decir su apellido, porque tuviste varios atreves del tiempo en que nos conocimos… pero con solo decir su primer nombre, Verónica…. sabíamos de quien se trataba. Tu lucha por la vida se reflejó en tu amor por tu familia y tu comunidad, y eso nadie lo podrá negar. Lo que más me gustaba era escuchar las historias de tu vida, y saber lo mucho que nos unía, nuestro deseo de mejorar el futuro para nosotras como mujeres Latinas, como la de toda la comunidad. Siempre estabas dispuesta a ayudar en cualquier trabajo que desarrolláramos, nunca me dijiste que no tenías tiempo, al contrario, el tiempo siempre lo hacías para la comunidad. Te voy a extrañar mi Hermana…. Sigue alumbrándonos con tu pasión y amor donde quiera que te encuentres…. Mi Verónica.

Translation:

I met you as we knew each other back then… Latin Mothers, warriors, thirsty to help our people in the community. We wanted our people to succeed, and we demonstrated that with our own examples. We studied and graduated from college, so that other Latina mothers could see that it could be achieved. We left family or friend relationships if there was abuse, mistreatment, or discrimination, and we supported women victims of domestic violence. We had no phones, no computers, no email, and no social media… Our connection network was passion, struggle, and life! That united us like an umbilical cord. To maintain our mental health, we met every so often, just because, for coffee, breakfast, or a drink … We didn't need a reason to see each other, and each encounter fed our souls more to continue helping our people. There was an exchange of admiration for each other, and our stories were intertwined with our community work. She, my sister, my partner in struggle, my Veronica…. She didn't need to say her last name, because she had several since we met… but just by saying her first name, Veronica…. We knew who it was. Your struggle for life was reflected in your love for your family and your community, and no one can deny that. What I liked most was to hear the stories of your life, and to know how much it united us, our desire to improve the future for us as Latina women, as the whole community.

You were always willing to help in any work we developed, you never told me that you did not have time, on the contrary, you always made time for the community. I'm going to miss you, my sister.... Keep lighting us up with your passion and love wherever you are.... My Veronica.

Her adoptive grandkid, Camilo Bonilla-Moyano

We lost someone very close to us, someone who was always there for others, helping in any way she could. Her advice and company was something I really enjoyed. We would go out to eat and we shared so much through the years that it's hard to believe it has come to a sudden stop. Something I will always tell myself is that even if her candle has gone out, the memories of the light will never vanish.

Her adoptive grandkid, Alexandra Rivas Reyes

Veronica Martinez was one of the strongest women I have ever met. She was there for me when I felt like nobody else was there for me. She was the best adoptive grandma I could ever ask for. She did so much for me and I will never forget that. I'm very grateful for having the opportunity in life to have met someone like her and have her in my life. She was amazing in every way someone could be. She understood me and always made sure I was okay. She also supported me when I would want to do something. She would encourage me to do the things I wanted to do. Her laugh and her smile were pure. She was something so pure and I will never forget that.

Wela would always be there for anyone when they needed her. In the summers when she would pick me up and take me to her house. I would just stay there all day. They were the most fun days ever. Almost every day of that summer I was with her having the best times. She would give me the best gifts and I am so very grateful for everything that she did for me while she was here with us. Any time I was sick at school and my parents couldn't pick me up she was there at the door ready to take care of me.

She was my Wela and I will never ever forget her.

As I complete this chapter, the family saga with cancer diagnosis continues. In June 2023, my mother's husband has now been diagnosed with

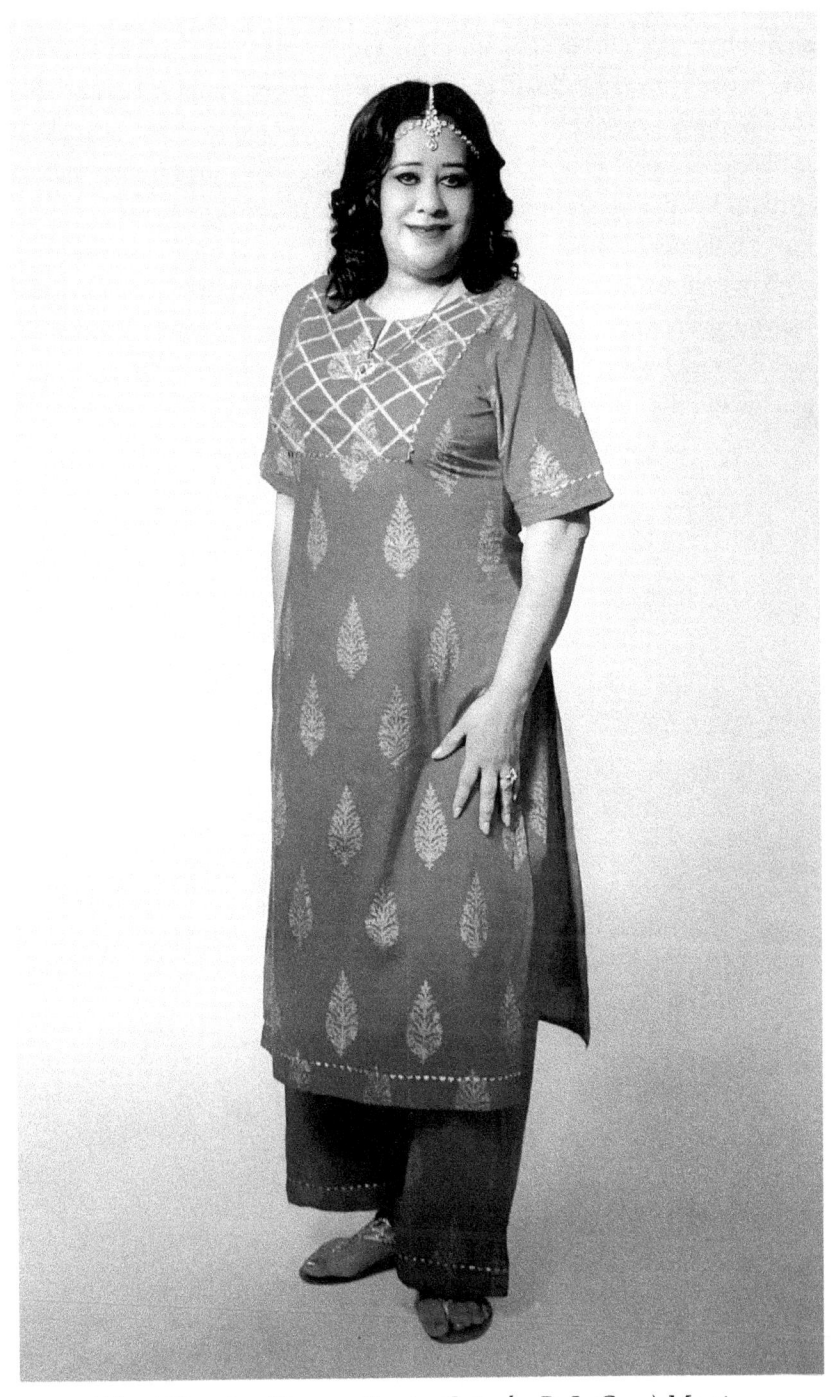

(Alma) Veronica (Guerra, Berrio, Caicedo, DeLaCruz) Martinez

stomach cancer. His first appointment with his oncologist will be after the due date of this book. I will go with him for moral support because that is what my Ma would have wanted. All I can think now is will he make it to the release of this book? Does my mom see how much he is suffering without her that she's coming back for him? Are we going to use the same hospice? Funeral home?

My final words to my Mother, Mami, Ma, Wela, Best Friend. I will see you again when I get to where you are. I know you will be waiting for me. Because I will always choose you to be my Ma in every lifetime from here on out. I can't wait to feel your embrace once again. Tu Reina Te Amo.

—*Jennifer Aracely Berrio Ortiz*

CHAPTER 3

The Last Year

In Loving Memory of Bob Tordoff, My Guy
September 3, 1957 – December 10, 2018

By Leslie Tordoff

2018 was a spiraling year of events. It was a year that I will never forget. It was a year that I had to say good-bye to my husband who was my lover, my best friend, my guy. It was a year that I had to let Bob go.

In January, Bob took better care of himself by eating well and exercising regularly. He enjoyed researching Rhode Island to uncover off-the-beaten-track trails that he could go hiking or ride his bike. No matter where he went, he would bring home a rock and explain to me the unique areas he had uncovered. He even created a rock garden in the front yard with which he would share his adventures with our neighbors. Bob was a special person.

February was a great month. Bob and I went to St Thomas. I look back at our time together and I am very disappointed in myself for putting him second to my work. If only I knew that our time was limited, I would have done things differently. When we returned home from St Thomas, Bob had his yearly check-up. All his hard work in changing his eating habits and exercising paid off. He lost weight and his cholesterol levels were the best ever. He was so proud of himself. I remember him telling me how his doctor said he wished his health was as good as Bob's. If only the doctor knew that there was a time bomb inside of Bob which was going to take him down.

In March we found out that our daughter Kim was going to have her first baby. Bob was so thrilled that his little girl was going to have a little one. This would be our third grandchild. Our son, Rob was already blessed with two boys, Blaise, and Rocco. We were so lucky to have a healthy, happy, and loving family.

The next few months passed very fast. Then in May, Bob started to have back pains. He blamed it on his exercise routines. So, he decided to cut down on the miles he went biking.

June was our annual family vacation in Little Compton, RI. The house we rented was right on the beach and all the kids came. If only we knew this was our last vacation together. During this week Bob started to have symptoms of a slight fever every day. He would take Advil, but the fever always came back. He did not want the kids to know that he was having back pains and the pain was causing him discomfort. He did agree that when we returned home from our vacation, he would make an appointment to see the doctor. This was when our lives changed and the hell began. The doctor did not understand what was going on with him. Several appointments were made for tests that all came back negative. The frustrations were waiting for appointments and waiting for test results which came back negative. Bob was getting very frustrated. I could see the pain on his face, things were getting worse. This was very overwhelming for our family.

In July, Bob started to have a hard time swallowing and eating solid foods. His doctor decided to schedule Bob for an MRI. I remember Bob saying before the appointment that he did not have a good feeling about this test. A few days passed and we were informed that he had a tumor on his esophagus. The doctor scheduled an appointment for a bronchoscopy in August to perform a biopsy on the tumor. After the biopsy was completed, we again needed to wait for the results. The next day I was working from home and Bob came into my office saying he was having a hard time breathing and coughing up blood. I quickly called 911 which took him to Miriam Hospital. This was when our lives would never be the same.

He was admitted and several doctors started to get involved in reviewing all his test results trying to diagnose his symptoms. It was then he was diagnosed with esophagus cancer, and he was in stage IV. The doctors immediately started chemotherapy treatments in the hospital hoping to slow down the cancer on his esophagus and liver. Then they immediately set him up with Total Parenteral Nutrition (TPN).

Bob was so positive. It was like a bad dream. I did not know what to say to him. I would just look into his eyes and ask him, what do you need me to do for you. But his health just started to decline. He kept his diagnosis to himself at first. It was later that I realized there were a lot of things Bob kept to himself. He always would have his conversations with his doctors alone. He did not want anyone to interfere with his decisions that he needed to make. Bob was finally released from the hospital and he would continue with his chemotherapy visits and TPN processes. We had visiting nurses in and out of our home. They all were very professional and kind. They encouraged us to ask them questions and, if needed, to call them anytime.

It was in September Bob had a follow-up with his cancer doctor and this time he asked me to go with him. Usually, he wanted to do these visits on his own. It was during this visit I found out the truth of his diagnosis. It was during this visit I was told from his cancer doctor that Bob only had three months to live. It was then I found out that he decided to do the chemotherapy treatments so he could live a few more months longer to have the opportunity to see his little girl have her baby that was due in November. It was so overwhelming; I could hear them talk but I could not speak. I just sat there and listened to this horrible story of what he has been going through on his own and what was ahead of him. I could not look into his eyes. I did not know what to do. Here was my guy, my love of my life, and he only had six months to live if he was lucky.

I started a journal to keep track of his treatments, making sure he took his medicines on time and worked with the visiting nurses at home. This became my second full time job. I know that this needed to be done to make sure we did everything to help him. Every morning when I got up, I would review the journal before I started work, I made sure we both were on the same page as to what needed to be accomplished that day. This was very overwhelming, I needed to make sure the journal was correct so there would be no issues relating to his treatments, medicines, doctors, and nurse visits.

The visiting nurses would take their time with Bob in discussing what they were doing and why. They even spent time with me, teaching me how to change the nutrition bags, cleaning the connections, and changing the intravenous bag. I kept telling them that I am not a nurse and they kept telling me I would be fine. Just take your time with each process and if there were any issues just call them and they would be right over, no matter what time of day it was. They were incredible. Kim would take Bob to his chemotherapy treatments. Rob would stop by at night, after work and make him laugh. He really enjoyed his time with Kim and Rob.

Bob and I would spend hours just sitting together and talking about anything and nothing. I never cried in front of him. He had enough to deal with; he did not need a crazy wife crying on his shoulders.

In October after several chemotherapy treatments the doctor scheduled an MRI to see how things were progressing. The results were in, Bob and I went to the doctors in hopes of receiving good news. It was then we found out that the tumor on the esophagus was reduced and the TPN process could stop. This was great news. But the cancer continued to be aggressive and was growing even faster than expected in his liver and kidneys. At this point chemotherapy was not working. He mentioned to Bob that there was a new clinical trial treatment that was going to start at the end of November and that he was a good candidate. This was very frustrating; how could chemo treatments only help with the esophagus tumor? I was numb, tears started to roll down my cheeks. First, we get good news, then we get the bad news, and maybe there might be an ending to this horror we have all been living. Bob was so brave and excited that there were still options on the table. He looked at me and said I need to sign up for the clinical trial. He stated that it might be too late for him but maybe they will learn something from his cancer that will help others.

It wasn't until October, I told my best friend Jane Pace, what was going on with Bob. Jane is a full-time volunteer for the Gloria Gemma Breast Cancer Foundation Team. Gloria was her aunt. Jane and I have been friends for over twenty-five years. She is a very special person. There are very few people in this world like her. She would give a hand to anyone in need. Jane opened her heart and arms to me. She was so supportive. She would call me almost every day and encourage me to be strong during this time. She would tell me stories about this ugly monster, cancer. She would say to me you need him to be strong and positive to fight this evil. She would send me prayers and tell me stories of cancer survivors and how they were coping with this disease. She gave me strength and courage to get through each day. I love her dearly.

In November Bob was eating food again so we decided to celebrate

Thanksgiving a week early since Kim's due date was on Thanksgiving Day (November 22nd). It was a great day at our house. We all sat around the table talking about the fun times we had, Kim being pregnant and giving birth in a few days. No one spoke about cancer, doctors' appointments, and the clinical trial treatments that were scheduled to begin the following week. The room was full of love and laughter. It was like old times. It was so good to see him happy and eating all his favorite foods, especially the cheesecake from Wright's Dairy. He ate the whole thing…happiness is….

Kim had her baby on Friday, November 23rd. I was lucky that Kim and Eric asked me to help with the birth of their first child (Winter Rose). Kim was in labor for over thirty hours. The labor room was so cold I had to wear my winter coat to keep warm. Kim was in a lot of discomfort; her contractions were strong and her cervix was not dilating as fast as she wanted. She did not want any medication and wanted to have natural childbirth… so they were trying everything and the last few hours she decided to take the drugs. Thank God. I just hated to see her suffer.

Once they gave her the Epidural, she fell asleep for a few hours. What an experience. All I kept thinking about was Bob at home. I was worrying about him, worrying what my life would be without him, and how this new little angel might not have the opportunity to meet him and get to know this fabulous man. Once Winter Rose was born and both were fine, I called Bob to give him the great news. He was so happy.

Bob had an appointment later that same day at the hospital to take blood and check all his vitals, since Monday, November 26th he was going to start the clinical trial treatments. He told me that he wanted to stop by to see Kim and Winter Rose before his appointment. He was so happy. It was such a beautiful feeling to feel all the love in this room. It was priceless. I could see Bob was very weak and he did not want to hold the baby. I could see the concern on Kim's face. He sat on the edge of the bed with Kim and kept touching Winter Rose's hands. It just wasn't fair that Bob could not hold his new granddaughter. If only we knew this was the last time we were all going to be together.

Bob and I left Women and Infants and took a short ride to Rhode Island Hospital; he did not look good. Neither one of us were talking. It was almost like we knew something was wrong. After they took his vitals and reviewed the results, they admitted him into the hospital. The doctor said that he was too weak to take part in the clinical trial. I could see the disappointment on his face, my heart broke, I realized the end was near. The evil cancer was winning. He never came home again, but he did get his wish to see his little girl with her little girl.

It was December 10th at 2:00 am that I got the call from the hospital that I needed to come in, things did not look good for him. It was hard to make the calls to Kim and Rob informing them of the situation. I was numb and felt disappointed with life. I could not feel anything. It felt like I was in a bad dream, that this was not real. I was driving the car to the hospital and it felt like the car was driving itself. I could not feel anything. The hardest part was trying to get into the hospital. All the doors were locked. I remember trying the door and saying out loud, "you got to be kidding me, I need to get in." Out of nowhere this security man came running to the door and opened it.

Kim, who just gave birth only few days ago, was breastfeeding the baby. So, the baby had to be close to her. She was able to get her father-in-law to meet her and Eric at the hospital. He was an angel. He would drive Winter Rose around the hospital in his car and call Kim when the baby was really fussing. Kim would go down to the car, feed the baby, and come right back up to be with her dad.

During Bob's last few hours of life, we were all at his bedside. The nurses were very kind and understanding. They kept coming in and updating us on his vitals and informing us it was not much longer. We just sat there in silence until he took his last breath. I could not believe how I felt his life leaving his body. At that moment the tears stopped, it was like he was over us helping us to understand what was happening to him and he was going to be okay. The doctor came in to pronounce his time of death at 10:05 am and the nurse told us to stay as long as we needed. We all sat there and talked about him, this amazing man, and how much he had suffered the last few months. I could not believe how peaceful we all felt.

Another hard part was to plan his celebration of life. At his bedside I called the undertaker and left a message. Within minutes they called me back and told me they would be there shortly. We stayed until we were told that the undertaker was here to pick him up. We did not want him to be left alone. A few hours later we were at the funeral parlor planning his celebration of life. What an experience that I will never forget. We went into their office, and they had a big screen TV on the wall which was linked to their laptop computer. The first words were we are very sorry for your loss and let's bring up packages that you can select from. I looked at both Kim and Rob with shock…Packages? What do they mean? You select a package deal to celebrate your loved one's life. I just lost the love of my life a few hours ago and now I need to pick out a package deal that will celebrate his life. I don't know how people can deal with this. One of the questions they asked us was how many people you think will be attending the event. I told them that Bob did not want anything in the newspapers because he felt if they knew him, they would be there.

Bob did have a few other requests that he told me a few weeks before he pass, he did not want to wear a tie nor a suit, and he did make me promise to have a luncheon after the event, he told me the old people need to be fed. Everyone was so supportive.

I could not believe he was gone. Why did he have to leave us. It just was not right. It did not feel real, I did not feel real. I just kept myself moving forward to get everything ready to celebrate Bob's life. I would be sitting in the living room waiting for him to walk through the door. I felt like he really was going to walk through the door. I did not believe he was gone. How could this be real. It was only a few months ago he was so happy and healthy. My heart was aching for him. We spent the next few days selecting pictures of our family to tell his story. It was a nice way to remember Bob during this difficult time. It made us laugh and talk about all the good times we had together. We selected Frank Sinatra songs to be played, Frankie was his favorite singer. The last song to be played would be "I did it my way".

He was a remarkable person; he had a big heart and always knew when someone needed a bear hug. The day of his celebration of his life I told the funeral parlor again, I did not know how many people would be attending. But to our amazement the place was packed. We could not believe all the people who came to show support and express their love for him.

One of the things Bob told us was that he did not want us to cry at his funeral. He said it was not the place or time. He wanted us to be strong together. I did ask a few of his friends that I thought would have been willing to say a few words about Bob but they all said this was not something they could do. I wanted to make sure everyone knew what a great amazing man he was so I did the honors in honoring him for the last time. I wanted everyone to know about his younger years of where he went to school, and how we met when I was sixteen playing tennis at the public courts in Pawtucket, RI. He was a Gauge Engineer. His work made him a world traveler, visiting many countries over the years.

Raising our two children together was the best time. We both worked and sometimes our vacation times did not line up together. But this did not stop him. He would take Kim and Rob on day trips to Block Island, the beaches, and the zoos when they were small. He would even spend one-on-one time with Blaise, our grandson, picking him up for the day, going out to lunch, bike riding, and learning how to use tools from hammers to drills. They both had the best time ever by being together. I read the Golden Heart Stopped Beating poem by Melissa Fox-Austin. The whole event was beautiful, and I knew he was with us, and I know we made him proud.

During our many conversations Bob and I had there were only a few things he wanted to make sure I promised to do… Do not cut the lawn, let the lawn man do it, he does a better job than you. Do not shovel the driveway, you are getting too old to do this work, let the plow man do his job. Do not stop the cleaning service since she really needs the job. And don't forget to drop off my library books.

I have held up to all his requests. Dropping off his library books was the best request. I went to the Cumberland Library just a few days before Christmas. I could not believe all the hundreds of decorated trees honoring loved ones on the library grounds. It was so peaceful and beautiful. I spent the time walking around the trees to notice all the special messages that were left by loved ones. When I got home, I asked Kim to investigate this event and how we could obtain a tree for Bob next year. Ever since then we have decorated a tree honoring him. It was the greatest feeling ever. To be able to honor him every year at Christmas. It allowed us to celebrate his life together. The location of where the trees were was right next to his hiking path, a place he always loved to go. He loved nature. We all make ornaments; the best ones were the ones that fed the birds. These were usually created by Laura and the boys. We even hung family pictures.

Now I must deal with being alone. I do not want to be a burden to the kids. They have their own lives. My friend Jane kept telling me you are not alone, look for the signs from him and have an open mind. She always says believe beyond what your eyes can see, signs from heaven will show up to remind you. Love never dies. Jane was so right. I kept an open mind, and I did see signs. There are times when I would move around the house and for a brief second, I would smell him. I would stop in my tracks in hopes of being able to continue to smell him. But it never happened. These signs made me feel warm inside. It gave me a moment of comfort. It felt like he did remember me and he was looking over me. I felt special to have that opportunity to be with him one more time. One time my alarm went off for no reason, another time my front doorbell kept ringing, and even my lights would flicker in the house.

In June 2019, I booked the same house in Little Compton for our family vacation. This was Bob's favorite place. While we were there, I asked Kim and Rob to write a letter to him to say whatever was in their hearts. Then we lit a fire outside and the three of us read our letters out loud. Each of our letters talked about all the fun times we had with him. How he always told us to do our best and to look into the mirror and say you did your best each day.

In my letter I talked about how he left us too soon. How I will miss our bike rides and long walks. I will miss our time traveling together. I asked him how I am going to live without you. We were just getting ready to start our lives over again now that it was only the two of us. I asked him how am I going to survive? After we each read our letter, we threw it into the fire pit. It was the best thing we did to honor and remember him. As the letters were burning it felt like we were able to say things to him that we could not when he was alive. It was hard for us to tell him that we loved him because if we did tell him how we felt, we would just cry. We did not want him to see us crying since he was dealing with so much. We felt like we needed to be strong for him and not show him how weak we really were. Wondering what we will do without him. We did not want to be selfish.

After we were done, we looked up into the sky and there was a square rainbow above us. We wish one of us would have had their cell phone to take the picture, but we did not want to move since we wanted to enjoy this beautiful rainbow that we know came from him.

My friend Jane always looked after me. She asked me to volunteer for some of the Gloria Gemma Breast Cancer Resource Foundation events, which I did. She thought about me when they had Weight Watchers meetings at the Foundation. This is when I started to get to know Maria Gemma Corcelli, Executive Director of the Gloria Gemma Breast Cancer Resource Foundation. Both of these women have been through so much through this organization. To listen to their stories of all the women that have touched their lives really touched me. I am so honored to call them my friends.

In March 2020 COVID hit. This was awful, everything was shutting down, and this was the time I needed to get out and try to figure out how to live life on my own. But we were all on lockdown and no one understood what was happening or how long this was going to go on. There was no more face-to-face contact with anyone. Even taking walks around the neighborhood, everyone would run away or cross the street to avoid eye contact. My gym closed, I worked from home, shopping was done online, and all I did was eat. Eating made me feel good for a short time each day. Food was a way I coped with my grief. I gained thirty pounds and did not care about myself. I lost sight of who I was and was feeling very sorry for myself. Who did I need to look good for these days? I felt alone. I would stare at his picture and say to him, why did this have to happen to us. We were just starting to have fun adventures, just the two of us again.

Jane and Maria suggested that I join the Gloria Gemma Book Club in June 2020. They both encouraged me to get involved with people and get out there and live life.

I volunteered for Gloria Gemma Breast Cancer Resource Foundation's Flames of Hope. Jane and Maria even signed me up for Gloria's Warriors Dragon Boat Race Team. I told them I would try anything once. This was a great workout and it got me to spend time with people again.

In August 2022 Maria asked me to participate in ScART painting event. This experience was inspirational. Everyone at this event had been through so much. Attending this event made me realize I am not the only one who had hidden scars from cancer.

Maria encouraged me to join Gloria Gemma's Embracing Grief Support Group. Here I met other individuals who were going through the same horror of losing a loved one to cancer. Shakay Kizirian was a grief counselor who ran one of the Grief Support Groups. She is an amazing woman. She knew how to get everyone to open up, share their stories, and life events. It was encouraging and moving. Every time when I left the group sessions, I felt I was not alone. It was consoling. We all shared our stories in a reassuring environment.

The Grief Groups also gave me the opportunity to join Susan Lataille's Grief Support Group. Here is where I was encouraged by Maria to join the Share Your Loved One's Story group. These grief groups helped me to open up and tell my story. I was amazed with the similarities we all had in these group meetings. It felt good telling my story and I felt good hearing other's stories. Hearing their stories made me feel less alone. By telling my stories, I realized that I was not crazy with the way I was handling my grief. It felt like some of the weight that I was carrying was lifted. I learned that everyone grieves differently. It made me feel needed again as well, that what I was saying was helping them as much as they were helping me. In these groups I felt comfortable to share the signs that I experienced and received over the years from Bob. It was surprising to hear we all felt the same. Everyone was so supportive and nonjudgmental. We all miss our loved ones, and it was an incredible feeling for all of us to share our journeys.

I have learned that grief never ends. Every day I think about him. I get so jealous of seeing couples walking down the street or shopping holding hands, knowing that this will never be me again. Missing long walks and talking about my most inner vulnerable thoughts and feelings with him. To wonder if I am ever going to laugh again the way I used to laugh with him.

I need to constantly stay occupied so I can get through the day. Nights are still very hard and lonely. I am beginning to smile and say hi to strangers in the stores again. This does make me feel good, but it quickly fades away. I am trying to laugh again. I still do not laugh like I use to when I was with him. I keep telling myself one day at a time, that is all you can do. Do what you feel is good for you and try to enjoy life. It's hard for me to relearn how to rely on myself to be happy. I always had my husband. I joined a gym again, to help lose weight and feel good about myself. It's nice to get up in the morning and meet up with my gym friends and talk with them for an hour. I actually look forward to my gym days. I can see and feel the difference in my body, and it makes me feel good.

The kids and I are going to figure out how to spend more time together. It's always hard between their growing families. I don't ever want to feel like a burden on them but it's nice to at least talk to them on the phone. Even using FaceTime to interact with my grandchildren makes my day. The three of us took a trip to New York City for Bob's anniversary weekend. This was the best time ever. We talked about the good old times and celebrated the old man. We were able to put our walls down and be vulnerable with each other. Helping each other through our feelings and trying to understand what each of us was going through. We still do not understand why he was taken from us.

We know that it's important to keep living our lives and prioritizing spending time together as a family. Learning and realizing grief is a vicious cycle and understanding you cannot outrun it. Most days I can live with it but some days are just very overwhelming. Knowing that I have my family behind me helps me to get through the toughest of days.

All these events that I participated and volunteered in with Gloria Gemma Foundation helped me to fill a void in my life. I have met a lot of amazing people and I am slowly finding the strength within myself that it is okay to move forward. Jane and Maria are amazing and beautiful individuals and I don't know what I would have done without their help. They both keep encouraging and reassuring me that life will get better. I am so lucky to have them as friends. Thank you for being you.

Bob Tordoff

CHAPTER 4

Heaven Called You Home

In Loving Memory of Lisa M. D'Arezzo
November 19, 1968 – July 2, 2022

By Brittney L. D'Arezzo

December 28, 1992 I met my first best friend and my forever friend for the first time, my mom (Lisa D'Arezzo). My mom and I had a bond like no other. I was the rainbow/only child so not only did she have the title mom but she also the person who knew me better than I knew myself. My mom was also a stepmother to my sister Cheryl who was my dad's oldest daughter.

My mom had me at twenty-four, so she was one of the younger moms out of my friends. She was the mom all my friends went to, the mom who had a seven-passenger truck because she always had a car full and the mom who also went to concerts with us growing up! Lisa had to be the only mom who enjoyed a Lil Wayne concert or any concert she would take me to. She loved music. She was always singing no matter where or what she was doing. Besides music, she was your All-American sports girl. She loved the Patriots and a was Red Sox fan.

Lisa grew up in Braintree, MA with her parents, and older brother Billy, along with aunts, uncles, and cousins! She was the baby out of her and her brother. She was the daughter of the late John Costa (owner of Ferrara Meats in Providence), and late Marie Costa. They moved to Rhode Island when she was nine years old. She resided in Johnston and lived here till she passed. She lived with her parents, brother, and her Nanna Bell (her best friend). As she grew up, she eventually ended up getting her first "baby", her dog Biscuit whom she loved dearly.

If you ask anyone, including her cousins, they would tell you "Lisa was the tough one out of the crew. From fights, school suspension, and just always into something she shouldn't have been." You just didn't mess with her if you were smart.

My mom lived for nights and weekends in hockey rinks. Her brother traveled worldwide for hockey, and where he was, there was my mom. Even in the rinks she would find a way at times to be thrown out by fighting with the referee. She always wore his uniform Number Six proud and as she would call it, her lucky number.

Unfortunately, later in my mom's teen years, an unexpected tragedy turned her prime years into a nightmare. Her dad, my grandfather John who was only thirty-eight years old, was hit by a drunk driver that led him to be a paraplegic. He was paralyzed from the neck down. I remember my mom telling me what their schedules would look like to help out with her dad when John (his nurse) went home for the night and before arriving in the morning. She was a daddy's girl. Even being in a hospital bed she kept him on his toes.

When my mom talked about her childhood, my heart broke for her. She had always told me she experienced a lot of heart aches in her childhood. Hearing those words brought my heart so much pain because she didn't deserve that. She did not have a bond with her mother like she and I had. You always need your mom in life no matter how old you are and sadly my mom could not always count on hers.

My mom graduated Johnston High class of 1987. From there, she tried hairdressing school but that did not last long. It was not for her. During those years she met my dad Louis. They met at Dunkin Donuts on Atwood Ave and then the rest was history. She left Dunkin Donuts and worked at Providence BluePrint for many years. She met her "bestie" as she would call her Rosemary. These two were the friends that turned into family.

On June 23, 1990 my parents got married. My grandfather had gotten his wish. He was able to walk his little girl down the aisle and dance with at her wedding. But mostly, I know she was so thankful to have her dad at her wedding and "dance" with him in his wheelchair. I am sure she would have loved for him to spin her on the dance floor as they danced to their father/daughter dance.

She spent months in the hospital visiting because that was the only way to see her dad when he was admitted. Unfortunately, a year after she was married in April of 1991, he passed away. He had always wished for my mom to give him a grandchild or, as he hoped for, a "little Ruby." Sadly, I was born the following year and never got to meet my grandfather.

When I was five, she started working at RIPTA where she worked for over twenty-five years up until her passing. It's ironic to me that I am now working at RIPTA also in the same position she started in. Lisa was a devoted worker who enjoyed her job and what she did. She also worked at Pocasset Bay Assisted Living in Johnston as a server with my aunts. My mom enjoyed this job a lot. She worked one night during the week there and on the weekends. All the residents loved her. They would sit and wait for her. Her heart was made of gold and was made for that job. She loved making their day, or just sitting with them and letting the residents know how much she really cared about them.

My mom was an amazing person who put others before herself. Between holding down my house, working full time, and taking care of my grandmother, she always did it all with a smile. When she had time to herself, on a hot summer day you could have found my mom down on Salty Brine Beach with an ice coffee in her hand! If you knew my mom, you knew she saved all her vacation time for the summer, a week for my birthday, and two weeks for a family trip. Or you could find her planning our next family vacation to a tropical island as we did yearly.

Our last family vacation was 2019. We went to Aruba! That was her dream trip. Well, she made sure we did it right this time around. We stayed there for over two weeks. I am so glad we made that trip. Not knowing that would be the last family trip we would take. We made so many great memories on that vacation as we did each trip, but this one was different. Aruba, known as "One Happy Island" made sure we were nothing but happy and enjoyed our family and friends' company. March of 2020, Covid hit. The world shut down and there was no traveling, the world was on lockdown. I remember her saying "As soon as we can travel again we are out of here!" We renewed our passports and were planning to go back to Jamaica, another trip she really enjoyed. Sadly, no one knew what God had in store for us in the upcoming months.

Fast forward to 2021, the year my family and my life changed in ways we would never have imagined. My mom was healthy, never had any health conditions besides high blood pressure. She always joked with my dad and me. She said we were the reason for that and her taking pills twice a day for it! Walking was her passion and she loved kickboxing.

July is when it all started. My mom had started noticing changes in her vision and seemed to develop headaches a lot more frequently than normal. She went to the eye doctor first to make sure it wasn't her prescription, but it wasn't her eyes. They were fine. From there we noticed she was forgetting a lot more. I remember joking with her, asking her "Are you losing it, Mom?" How horrible I felt about that once we found out what was wrong.

I'll never forget this day as long as I remember. It was a Sunday afternoon and her driving was off. We went shopping as that was one of our favorite things to do together. She drove and my life had flashed before my eyes several times that day between running red lights, stop signs and just being in a fog. I knew something was not right because we were on roads she drove on daily. Later that day she still didn't seem "right." We went out for Sunday dinner as a family as we always did. How she was acting made me concerned. I was scared and nervous as I noticed physical changes so I immediately stopped at the fire department to have them check her out. After doing a full assessment, they told my dad and I to go home and get what you need. We are going to rush her to Rhode Island Hospital, and meet to us there. I went numb. I didn't know what was wrong besides her blood pressure being high and her left side was a little weaker than normal.

When we arrived at Rhode Island Hospital there was a Neuro team waiting for her. They immediately did a CT scan of the brain. Well, my mom never cries. We didn't call her a bull for no reason. She was one of the toughest people I ever met. When I walked in she was hysterical. All she could say was "a lot of fluid on my brain." I froze and just looked at my dad in hysterics.

Of course, they admitted her right away. Two long days down in the emergency room. The next day they did an MRI of the brain. That is when our family's world turned into a nightmare that we could not escape.

Dr. Steven Toms came in to introduce himself and to go over the results. I'll never forget these words as long as I'm alive: "I am so sorry, I wish I had better news. Unfortunately, your mom and your wife Lisa has a grade four aggressive brain tumor called Glioblastoma that is cancerous." Talk about black out. I said no, not the C word. I lost it I started screaming at Dr. Toms because it couldn't be true. My mom? But she's healthy! Why? How? I looked over to my dad who was holding my mom in hysterics as I laid in her arms because family is everything to him. We didn't have time to waste as the tumor had developed shy of eight weeks and had grown so quickly. He booked her brain surgery for July 26, 2021.

The weekend before her surgery my mom had plans that she refused to let bring her down. We had a girls' weekend planned at Foxwoods for her bestie's birthday. Crazy right? But she lived that weekend to the fullest! Monday came. I had dreaded that day. Due to the pandemic going on, the hospitals were not allowing anyone in but the patients. Little did they know that day, their policy was about to change. I had met a nurse who was so kind, caring, and was probably overhearing me yell. She saw how upset my dad and I were. She could only let one person in with her until they prepped her. My dad sat with her. They told me surgery would be about seven to eight hours. Talk about the longest eight hours of my life. I remember just staring at my phone all day waiting for 444 to pop up on my screen. I will never forget I finally received the call from Dr. Toms at 6:10pm. Her surgery went well! They removed the majority of the tumor, and my mom was up and walking in a day.

One thing about my mom, she was always determined, and nothing was going to keep her down! We knew we had a long road ahead as a family but as my mom always said, "There is someone always worse off than us, we got this." She started radiation treatments and handled them like a champ along with chemotherapy orally at home. In between radiation and chemo, we would have regular follow up visits at the APC building. I didn't do well with those. My uncle usually always came to help us.

I tried to not let my anxiety and nerves get to me but it never worked. I passed out almost every visit we had. I remember her last day of radiation. We were all so excited and I'll never forget her ringing the bell! Tears of joy and excitement just ran down our faces. We had a follow up about two weeks later, and the tumor had shrunk, and things were looking great!

We ended the summer just how we normally would every year by the pool with great friends and family. November came and we celebrated her birthday as always, but never did I imagine that it would be the last one with her. We brought in the new year with hopes of a better year, positive thoughts and looking into a vacation eventually.

Two months into 2022 things started to take a turn for the worse. My mom was starting to lose her balance a lot more, falling frequently, and started to have seizures. Station One fire department became more than first responders and more like family we saw on the regular. Especially the guys on Rescue 1. Rescue 1 was the crew that always showed up to every call and even would just help me get my mom up the stairs. To say they were amazing was an understatement.

They scheduled another MRI, and when they called and said we need to go over the results I became choked up instantly. I knew calls from the neurologist were never a good thing. Well, I was right. Unfortunately, the tumor had traveled to the back of her brain, sitting on the nerve that controls her gross motor. Chemo treatment became infusions and a lot stronger to try to get the tumor under control. I feel guilty because my dad would take my mom to chemo. I tried once but I became so upset and could not handle or accept her sitting there for hours tired, cold, and completely drained. Unfortunately, treatment would only work for a couple weeks as the tumor grew and shifted.

As my mom was diagnosed and went through treatments, I felt like this wasn't my life. How could it be my life? My mom was fine then all of a sudden, our worlds changed in a blink of an eye. There were so many questions I had that no one could ever answer. Why her? Why a cancer that was not curable? I never told my mom because I tried to be strong for her. I cried every night from fear. I feared my mom dying, the fear of the days going by so quickly and only getting shorter for us to be together and losing my best friend. I didn't know how I could live without her, how I was going to function, just how I could ever be the "same" again. I lost a lot of weight during this time. I couldn't eat. I was so sick over the whole thing.

My dad's heart was shattered. He said it every day, it should have been him going through this not my mom because he was so much older. He let his health go. He wouldn't leave my mom even with the nurses because he was scared. He never left the house. Some days his emotions got the best of him, especially when it came to me. His anger built up and would be taken out on me, which was so hurtful at times. I was doing all I could caring for my mom, from bed baths, getting her out of bed alone, to her medications and some days he made me feel like I wasn't doing a good job or feeling the hurt he was.

The falls became more severe and almost daily. It broke my heart because by the first week in May she wouldn't go out anymore. She was too embarrassed, and it took all the energy she had in her. My mom NEVER sat home. She was a woman on the go 24/7.

The end of May, she was rushed to the hospital because she had another seizure. They admitted her but unfortunately the tumors had stopped responding to the treatments. Her oncologist came in and it was more bad news after another. More words that I couldn't even grasp my head around. "Does Lisa have a will made out?" I learned that day that I would never get thrown out of a hospital if I didn't when those words came out of his mouth.

He began to explain to me and my family that unfortunately in time my mom is just going to get worse and decline quickly. They asked where we would like to put my mom when they discharged her because she was going to be moved onto hospice. Well, my dad and I didn't even have to think where we were going to put my mom because the only place that she was going was home with us where she belonged. She was discharged a week later and was taken home by ambulance. All my close neighbors and friends were outside, waiting to greet her with balloons, and a celebration.

My dad and I had my mom home for about eight weeks with hospice care. I never had it in me to be a nurse, but I learned quickly. I prayed every day to God to give me strength because my mom needed us. My dad was my MVP! He sat with my mom around the clock and never left her side, especially during the day so I could try and work a couple hours. Even with my mom being on hospice, she never once complained and tried to stay positive. Her appetite was like no other. She would eat around the clock. Especially Allies Donuts! She listened more to music during this time, and fell in love with a singer who had also been diagnosed with cancer, Night Birdie. That gave her the strength and courage to keep fighting.

June 28th my mom was rushed back to the hospital due to passing clots. Little did we know, that was the last time she would ever be home and we would be a family of three. They always said you get your burst of energy before you pass and they weren't lying. Unfortunately, after the burst of energy disappeared, she declined rapidly. She was sleeping a lot. They had to force fluids in her, and watch her so she did not aspirate. I knew we were losing her when she asked me who I was. My heart shattered that day. I couldn't accept that her memory was fading and she didn't recognize me. But with a little hint she smiled at me and said "Brittney Lynn." We had a family meeting that afternoon and decided that we wanted her to be in a quiet, peaceful place.

Thursday night she was transported to HopeHealth Hulitar Hospice Center in Providence. They were all so amazing there. I could never thank them for taking such good care of my mom and making sure she was nothing but comfortable. My dad and I slept there for two days. We had our family and friends in and out to say their goodbyes because we knew it was only days that she had left. Friday was awful. I had never heard what they call the "death rattle" until that day. She was out of it. They had started giving her morphine every few hours to help with the pain she was experiencing when we rotated her or washed her up. Her breathing was heavy, her feet and legs started to turn purple and become cold.

Friday night, the nurses came in as they always did to rotate her and check her coloring. Well, they said they had never seen a patient play tricks on them until meeting my mom. Her color came back in her legs and the coldness had gone down. They said, "Lisa is on her time", and running the show. Saturday she was still in the same state. In the morning her coloring was the same from the night before. Around noon is when her legs became cold and color throughout her body was turning. The doctor has said it was a matter of hours. I didn't leave her side. I couldn't miss her taking her last breath. Even though hospice did say sometimes they will pass when you leave the room, so the loved ones do not have to witness the passing. I refused to let that happen.

I laid in her bed with her and talked to her. I know she could hear me. She squeezed my hand along with my dad's. We were even lucky enough that she opened her eyes quickly for us. I told her how much of an amazing mother she was, how much I loved her and told her it's okay. It was okay to let go. She was suffering and I couldn't be selfish to keep her here that way. The doctor did another check around 1:15. The purple and coldness was past her knees. It had come down to reality. We had no more time left with our queen.

We asked the nurse at the front desk to shut our door and not allow any more visitors. The room was filled with my dad, aunt, and uncle. Tears and silence filled the room. I remember being buried in her pillow, flooding it with tears. I could feel her heart slowing down. I will never forget feeling her take her last breath. When I couldn't feel it anymore, I jumped up. My aunt looked over at me and said I'm sorry honey, she's gone. The room became full of screams and hysterics. My best friend and my dad's one true love became our angel. She was taken from us too soon. She passed away at fifty-three years old.

July 2, 2022, at 2:58 pm life was never the same. I talked to her after she passed. The doctor told me hearing was the last thing we lose after we pass so all I could say was I love you over and over. The nurses let us have as much time as we needed with my mom. We sat with her for a while after she passed. As the nurses came in to clean her up, I stood up for the first time in hours. I collapsed. I passed out. I couldn't handle the reality that she was gone, gone forever. Nurses surrounded me with cold compresses and got me back up. That afternoon, a piece of my heart left me and my dad lost his beautiful wife and soulmate.

After that day of my mom passing, nothing seemed real. I felt as if I was in a daze. I was so numb I couldn't express anymore emotions. Going to the funeral parlor to organize the wake, funeral, and to pick out her casket was horrifying. I never had to do that before. I felt as though physically I was there, but mentally I couldn't process all that was being said. But I had to be strong. My dad couldn't handle it, so it was on me to make sure everything was perfect for our queen. I thought I was weird or crazy. Until my mom's cousin gave me a book called "Letting Go With Love." It explained all the grieving stages and processes. I couldn't sleep at night, couldn't think straight, basically was a mess waiting to burst. It took me a while to start grieving because three weeks after losing my mom, my grandmother (my mom's mom) passed away and I was the one who found her. Again, Station One Rescue 1 responded to that call. Those guys had been there through it all with me at this point.

I just couldn't understand why God kept knocking me down and why all this was happening to me. I was so angry, bitter, and never knew how many tears one can cry. Life just didn't seem to be getting better. In November, my dad started to make frequent trips in and out of the hospital due to his heart. The same rescue and guys were regulars again at my house. This became almost weekly.

The week of Christmas, I lost my job. At that point I felt I had hit rock bottom. The day after my thirtieth birthday, my dad had heart surgery. He faced more obstacles and ended up being there longer than expected. I felt defeated. I knew I was strong, but I was at my breaking point. I was lucky enough to have my village when I needed them most. During all this all I needed was the one person I turned to in life, my MOM and she wasn't there. That broke me even more.

Almost nine months later, and I am still grieving. Despite everything happening since my mom's passing, I have also had to go through all the "firsts" without her. Christmas was hard. That was her favorite holiday. But my dad was very sick on Christmas Day, so that kept me very busy. Mother's Day was unbearable. I cried from morning till night. I sat at the cemetery for hours that day. I could not believe that this would be how I celebrate her and holidays for the rest of my life. Every day I feel as though this nightmare is going to end, like it's not real.

Still grieving and going through so much, I was introduced to an amazing woman, Maria Gemma, known as the Gloria Gemma Foundation. My mom's friend of thirty years introduced me to her. Before my mom passed, she had raised enough money to be a torch carrier in the Gloria Gemma Flames of Hope Ceremony. She was so excited to be walking side by side with her friend Kristen! Kristen had introduced Maria to my mom through social media. My mom would message Maria often, and wanted to become involved with the foundation. As a family, we use to attend the Gloria Gemma Flames of Hope ceremony to support Kristen. The last one we attended as a family was in October 2021. Unfortunately, that did not go so well. My mom got sick. The lights and being overwhelmed caused her to pass out. I never thought I could run through the city as quickly as I did that night for medical attention.

Maria showed me the messages my mom had sent her telling her how beautiful the ceremony was, and how she was so overwhelmed and could not believe that she was now a warrior battling brain cancer. I couldn't believe Maria saved those messages, it meant a lot to me. My mom set up her fundraiser to be a torch barrier and hit her goal in less than forty-eight hours! Little did I know because my mom raised enough money, I would be able to carry the torch in honor of her. Her last wish would be fulfilled!

That night was emotional like no other. Friends and family gathered to celebrate my mom's life. I felt so honored to be able to be part of such a moving night, and keep my mom's wish and memory alive. The following day on Sunday, we had created a team in honor of my mom for the 5k. We had banners made, her favorite Allie's donuts, Mimosa of course, because I am always "extra"' as she would say! But most of all the people who loved her were there. Even the kids participated in the walk who she loved dearly. Especially her number one boy as she called him, Mekhai! The bond they had, no one was coming between them. Mekhai knew my mom as "Mama D" and the name stuck from an infant until she passed. That was her "grandchild" she never had. She loved taking him to their favorite date spot, Newport Creamery and having themselves a day.

Gloria Gemma has gone above and beyond with helping. Between books, gifts, offering to cook Thanksgiving dinner for my dad and I and the amazing opportunity for letting my mom's story live on forever. I was never one for counseling, but I was struggling so Maria told me to come to the group and she would be there to help me. So I did. It was hard, emotional and something I never thought I would be doing. But I am glad I did. I have met so many people that are going through the same thing as me, when I thought I was alone I met so many caring individuals.

What I have done since July 2nd to help me "LIVE" is that I just don't stop. More like I don't have the time to stop and relax. Staying busy just numbed the pain, rather than sitting and doing nothing. Being around my close circle helped me keep smiling on my worst days. I know this sounds crazy, but talking about my mom as if she was still here, and just about her helped me. I feel that when I do that, she is always with me. I made a promise that I would keep my mom's legacy alive and made sure her spirit lives on forever. So, with that being said, I had planned a few events this year to do just that. Both her and I LOVED planning events, so that brings a smile to my face knowing she would be so happy.

This past Memorial Day, on May 29th I hosted my first "Drive For A Cure" golf tournament in honor of my mom. That was an amazing day. A day filled with love, memories and great support all for our queen. We raised $4,444.50. All the proceeds were donated to the Rhode Island Brain & Spine Tumor Foundation in hopes for a cure. I knew that she had to be with us that day. Maria had let me in on a little secret that gave me goosebumps. Multiple fours are angel signs!

What did not help me was nighttime. I am an over-thinker. I found myself very upset at night just thinking about memories, looking back at old messages, wrapped in her favorite blanket just being very sad and trying to understand why God took my best friend. I'm not sure how I would say I learn to live during the grieving. For me, it's more of the numbness that just helps me get through the days. None of this gets easier, but only harder. I find as time passes, I am more emotional than when she first passed, sad, and a different version of who I was before she passed. At the end of the day, I have to keep going. After she passed, I had to step up quickly and take on more roles. Besides working full time, I am now the head of the household who takes care of my dad full time. I handle all his appointments, medications, and I have become his "nurse" as he would say. My mom was the definition of a housewife and did it all so my dad never had to, or had to learn how to keep a house running.

Who am I today after experiencing such a close loss? I am known as Brittney, Lisa's little twin. More and more since my mom has passed, I get told how much more I look like her, and act just like her. I am also a proud daughter. To hear all the kind words people have shared with me about my mom makes me push myself more and more to be half of the person she was. I am also stronger now than before. My mom always would joke with me and tell me how I was such a hot mess because I was always such an emotional person. Watch a love story movie, I'd cry. Come across old pictures of my grandparents, I'd cry. Forget home movies, she hid those on me, haha.

I still am emotional, but things don't upset me as much anymore. But almost a year later since my mom passed, I find myself struggling. I am a roller coaster of emotions. Trying to find myself in this world and be happy. That sounds so easy to some, but for me it's hard. Unfortunately, the mentality I now have and has grown so much overtime is this: who wants to be a part of my life and whoever doesn't, feel free to leave at any time. I have lost the most important person in my life, and nothing could hurt like that.

What I wish I knew was why all this happened. How did this all happen? But most of all if my mom is finally at peace. The last few days before my mom's passing was the most painful thing I've ever witnessed. The person laying in the hospital bed was not the mom I've known in my whole thirty years. She was struggling. She was uncomfortable, she couldn't breathe well. She wasn't awake. But most of all I wish I knew if she was able to understand all that I said to her lying next to her for two days. I meant every word I said to her and I hope she was able to hear me.

Grieving and losing my mom has changed me in so many ways. I was always grown and mature, but it matured me in a different way if that makes sense. I loved nail days, I still do, but it doesn't faze me if I miss an appointment or get them done. Material things don't make a difference to me anymore. I don't have to go run and buy what I see. None of that matters.

I also lost some people during my grieving process because "I had changed." I was so insulted when I was told that. But they were right. I changed, but not in a bad way. Instead of putting everyone else before myself I took a step back. I had told myself I was done being that person when it was only convenient or on other people's time when I go above and beyond for people constantly. My mom always told me, "The ones who love and give the most, always get hurt the most." Well, another thing she was right about.

I was turning thirty during all this, and I made a promise that I was keeping. This year was going to be all about me. It was going to be my year. I've learned life is too short. You want to take the chance, take it instead of wondering what if. You like that person you're crushing on, tell them. Go book that vacation you've been thinking of and make memories because at the end of the day memories last a lifetime. Even till this day, I am still grieving. All this is still raw and leaves me numb. I have gotten through all my "firsts" and I have to say those were the hardest things to overcome. I can say it never gets easier. I just have to keep going even though some days I just want to give up.

Words for My Beautiful Wife

"I lost my wife, my soulmate. Thirty-two years married, and thirty-five together. I never thought I would be without my wife. I miss her more and more each day and would do anything to be with her. Each day that passes only gets harder. I go daily to the cemetery to see her and grieve. I still am in love with you just like I was when I first laid eyes on you. I love you Lisa, my forever lady..."

Words from Her "Boo" as My Mom Called Jamie

Lisa was like a second mother to me from the day I was born. She always was a constant light who shined in all roles of her life. She was the type of person you didn't have to see every day to know at the end of the day she had your back and would be there for you no matter what you needed. The strength she had was admirable and I was always in awe of just how strong she was. I remember her going to chemo and radiation for hours then going out for a full day of errands or to work and of course making a stop at Dunkin for her iced coffee and never complaining.

I have a lot of great memories of Lisa but the one I remember the most is when I would sleepover and she would come in every night and sing to Brittney until she fell asleep. I remember not thinking much of it at the time but now that I'm a mother myself it showed how much being Brittney's mom meant to her and just how much she loved her.

Unfortunately, our time together was cut short but we are left with endless memories. One thing I can say about Lisa is nothing would take her spirit. If she wanted to do something, nothing would stop her. I want us all to keep her legacy alive. I know that's what she would want. Let her legacy live through your actions every day. Do the things Lisa loved and remind you of her. Take that walk, buy the person in front of you a coffee in her honor, or go on that trip. Life is short and tomorrow is never promised. I do know one thing, even on her worst days she lived her life and did what she wanted to the fullest. Let Lisa's legacy live through you each day.

Goodbye for Now
As dark gray clouds filled the air
I felt a warm wind blow through my hair
How could this be happening to my dear friend?
When would all of this suffering end?
Tears rolled down my cheek
I locked eyes with you but we didn't speak
We knew the fate that lay ahead
But my optimistic spirit had my heart misled
I knew this day would sadly come
But suddenly my heart dropped, I went numb
I remember a conversation we once had
Where you asked me to promise you to be strong, not sad
So, from that day on I am trying to remember
To fulfill the wishes of my dear friend born in November
Keep my daughter safe you whisper,
and I hope you know she will always be my sister
So as I say one final good bye
On that dreadful day back in July
There will be light when we meet again
And I'm looking forward to seeing you again, old friend

Lisa M. D'Arezzo

CHAPTER 5

She Wore It Well

In Loving Memory of Donna Genereux
July 24, 1956 – September 20, 2012

By Lisa Bastien

The Early Years

It all started July 24, 1956. My sister Donna was born. As long I can remember, Donna was an important part of my life. She was five years older than me, but it didn't matter. The pictures of her as a child before I was born showed a chunky little girl with a smile on her face. I was the kid sister who liked to be with her. She was never mean to me, at least I don't remember if she was.

I always remember that she never liked to go into the basement alone. Someone had to go with her, and many times it was me. I was just as scared as her, but I guess being the two of us, what could happen right? And the time I had always heard from my mother and stepdad that she had sworn one Christmas she saw Santa and stuck with that story forever.

I bought her the 45 of *Our House* by Crosby, Stills, Nash, and Young for Christmas one year. To this day every time I hear them, she comes to my mind. Easter was big for us because we used to drive to downtown Providence and have Chinese food at Luke's. It was down an alley near the City Hall. We would go there for many Easters that followed. I don't remember if it closed, or if we just started trying other restaurants.

In the summers, my parents rented a beach house at Ocean Grove in Swansea for a couple of weeks. The house was very tiny and full of people, but nobody cared, we were a close family. Those were good memories. She had her friends from the neighborhood and school that she would hang out with. It was the early 70's and they all thought they were cool wearing their hip huggers and short tops and of course all had the long hair that they ironed to keep it straight.

When she started driving, I would tag along with her. She didn't mind, which I always thought was so cool. She smoked cigarettes, and the only thing I didn't like driving with her was that the ashtray was always full and she only opened the window a crack to let the smoke out. She smoked cigarettes while she ate. It was the grossest thing, but she didn't care. Sometimes she would light one up with the one that she was going to put out.

Donna was great though because she let me wear her suede jacket with fringed sleeves which made me feel like a big shot! My parents worked so Donna had to step in and make the rest of us dinner and look after us until they got home. She grew up quickly. We grew up in a small house with six kids, parents, and one bathroom. I shared a bedroom with two of my sisters and Donna always stuck the gum she was chewing on the top of the headboard and just put it back in her mouth in the morning. She always had her hair rolled up with two huge curlers, one on each side of her head while she did her "boob" exercises to "make them bigger" while me and my sister Janice laughed at her. She never did have big boobs after all of that. Who knew that smoking cigarettes and doing her boob exercises would be her destiny? She did have boyfriends though and when she was seventeen years old, she got pregnant.

The Adult Years

Donna got married December 1, 1973. It was a quick wedding. My mother planning everything and we all got new clothes for the occasion. My sisters and I wore red dresses and had white bands in our hair. She and Harold moved into an apartment in Woonsocket and had my nephew Derek the following March. Donna was an adult at seventeen.

I would go with my mother to visit them at their apartment because I liked being with them. Harold ended up joining the Army, so they moved to Georgia. We became pen pals during that time. I still have some of the letters she wrote to me from 1977 and 1978. By then she had her daughter,

Jennifer. They ended up coming back home for good in 1978, which was great for me because I had my sister back instead of a million miles away.

Life was good, and our family just kept getting bigger and that little house just kept getting smaller, but it didn't matter because we were all together. We would still go out for Chinese food on Easter even as the family started to grow. Our family seemed to be tight-knit. We spent a lot of time together and in the summers we would all go camping together. We all had either tents or campers and always had so much fun whether it would be playing kickball or bingo or going out in the canoes. Life seemed great, everyone getting along and having fun and family seemed especially important. Time passed so quickly but life was good.

25 Years…Cancer & the Gloria Gemma Years

January 2008 was when Donna was diagnosed. It was all very confusing at first. She had an x-ray done because she had been having problems for years with these "cysts "on her breasts. Her doctor didn't seem to be concerned so nothing was ever done. Finally, a doctor drained one of them which she said was extremely painful. The x-ray seemed to show that she had stage IV breast cancer and Stage IV Lung Cancer as well. Two Stage IV primary cancers. Everyone was blown away. NO, THIS CANNOT BE HAPPENING, not to her, not to that wonderful smiley woman. She doesn't deserve this is what everyone was saying.

It was the beginning of her struggle to stay alive. It all happened so fast, the chemotherapy and radiation that went on for the next two years. She had a lobectomy and a bilateral mastectomy in September and November of 2008. Then Donna was diagnosed with bone metastasis and her hip was treated with radiation.

I was in a position where I could take her to her chemo treatments a lot of the time, which I gladly did. I would pick her up and off to Woonsocket we went. The office was set up with a row of chairs that the patients would sit on, and some would talk to us while others clearly didn't have the strength to want to talk. All the office staff were so nice and of course got to know her and her upbeat attitude every time she went. The routine of course was getting her set up to be juiced up for the next round. We would talk, watch TV, or read a magazine. I would always watch her while she rested so peacefully like there was no pain in her body. It was heartbreaking for me. I knew she was hurting but she would never show it.

After being there for a while I would ask what she wanted for lunch and go get it for us. One thing about Donna is she had a great appetite. Not so much on chemotherapy days but otherwise there wasn't anything she wouldn't eat. As our family always said, first one at the table, last one to get up. I would try and throw food out that was in her fridge but she wouldn't let anyone throw food away. She had an iron stomach. It was kind of funny.

Hours later, after her treatment for that day was over, I would take her home and sit with her for a little while as she lay on the couch with a blanket over her because she was tired, in pain, and needed rest. I would always leave crying because she meant so much to me and I hated what this was doing to her life. I was so angry, sad, and depressed, as was our family. I also knew that every time I left her house she would cry alone. Donna never wanted to cry in front of other people.

While all of this was happening to her, one morning, she woke up to see that her car had been stolen out of the parking lot. She called the police, and it didn't take long to find it in Providence, all chopped up. That was the end of that car. It was crushing when I heard the news, like she hadn't been through enough already.

The brightness in herself started to shine once she found the Gloria Gemma Resource Foundation and boy how they changed the life she was living through. They all welcomed her with open arms. Once she met the people from the Foundation, she lit up even more than she normally would. There's no question, she wasn't always happy even when she was in pain, but Maria Gemma opened the door to Donna to being with others with cancer. She embraced everyone and anything that came her way. She met so many people and they all were wonderful with her.

When she started losing her hair it was another sign of realism and it hurt to watch her lose her vanity but as usual, she was always a great sport and when she was ready, she walked into the Cotton Candy Boutique with clippers and my mother. She asked Jane Pace to shave her head. She was ready. Afterwards, she got Jane to also shave Gary Calvino's head which he agreed to. Apparently, they all laughed until they cried.

She participated in everything they had to offer. She felt extremely special around the Foundation, taking part in riding on the Pink Bus, going to the fashion shows, laughing a lot with Maria, Jane, and Gary. She adored all of them very much and met so many beautiful, wonderful women she called her friends.

The first Flames of Hope for us was in 2008. It was so emotional for everyone involved. My family had never attended one until this day. It was beautiful, the State House was lit up pink and there were so many activities going on. It seemed like everyone Donna knew in her life showed up on this incredibly special day for this incredibly special woman. We were all so proud of her on this day, showing how she fought this disease and was determined to continue that path. There were so many activities going on that day in Providence revolving around the Flames of Hope and many booths which had information and awareness tools for this disease.

All the torch bearers wore black and had their pink sashes on and huge smiles because it was the survivors' day to be honored and that they were kicking ass. I remember everyone crying as she was still in a wheelchair being pushed by my brother in-law, Tony with Jenn, my niece, Donna's daughter, who held the torch as they made their way in the procession from the State House down to the Water Fire.

She had been to hell and back at this point with all the surgeries and treatments she had gone through, but she was determined to be a part of this incredibly special ceremony in Providence. Afterwards, she participated in the breaking of the boards even from the wheelchair. It was extremely emotional, I'm pretty sure we all cried most of the night.

The atmosphere was very emotional, yet elation filled the air. The following year she was out of the wheelchair and using a walker. The pink out party at McCoy Stadium brought out a lot of people who watched Donna stroll out to the pitcher's mound to throw out the first pitch at the game. There were a lot of survivors who walked out with her, and I remember taking pictures from the stands telling anyone who would listen that it was my sister throwing that pitch out. Again, I was so proud of her for just being her happy self and touching everyone in her life. I am now the owner of that very hat she wore that night. I don't wear it much but when I do, I feel her.

The following year at Water Fire, Donna was able to walk and held that torch up as high as it would go. My sister Janice remembered thinking how Donna was so proud to be holding that torch by herself. It was easy to see the survivors were all remarkably close and supportive of each other. My sisters Janice, Lori, and I carried torches that year in support of Donna, it was such an honor to walk with her and feel the love that was coming her way.

There was also a 5K run/walk the following day which started with Donna's Divas as her team's name.

The first time we went to Sedona with Gloria Gemma Foundation was in 2010. My sister Lori and I went with Donna, not really knowing what to expect when we got there but quickly realizing it was going to be a journey within itself. The Red Rock and Vortexes almost put a spell on you. It is said that a vortex site brings about self-awareness and spiritual healing which I had witnessed the whole time we were there. The trip was definitely spiritual. I could feel it as soon as we got to the Enchantment Resort. The three of us were picked up at the airport and driven to this beautiful magical place.

I don't remember how many women came on this trip, but I do remember all of the camaraderie these women had for each other. There was a lot of hugging and kissing and crying and laughing. They were sisters. A Hacienda was reserved for anyone to go to meet up with other travelers from the Foundation. I remember tarot cards being laid out and spiritual reading material available. Maria had arranged meetings there and group activities for anyone who wanted to participate, which of course was all of us. Everyone would meet up in the mornings to have coffee and talk about each other's experiences.

The spa was quite a healing center as well. You could just hang out in your robe all day if you wished while you were there. It was quiet and easy to fall asleep if you wanted, maybe while reading a book or sitting by the fireplace. I remember sitting with Donna and Lori listening to everyone chatting and carrying on while in our robes. Donna was the life of any party. I felt so glad to have her as my sister and friend.

Arrangements had also been made to go into town and walk around and have lunch together at a restaurant. It was nice to be with all of these strong women, all battling the same disease but wouldn't know it when they were together. If someone wasn't feeling as well as the others, it was their purpose to help that person by being there for that person who was struggling just a bit more at any given time. What a wonderful intervention to watch these courageous and brave women.

There was a vortex right behind the spa and you can walk up these trails to get higher up to the Kachina Woman Rock and experience the energy if you are lucky enough. I think I wanted it so bad that I didn't feel it, but I saw women walking down who were crying because they had been moved by the energy. At any given time, you could hear the mountain men chanting and they would hand out red rocks shaped in hearts which was the coolest thing I've experienced in this form of being. Once I got to the top, I remember being peaceful and quiet, just observing and feeling everything, every sound that was around me. I listened to people talking and watched others sit in silence. I knew what they were feeling. The same thing I was, the feeling of sadness because I had someone in my life I adored battling cancer.

It was extremely hard to watch my sister go through this terrible disease but I knew I wasn't the only one to do so. There were many women there who also had loved ones to watch go through the same thing but in this instance they stood together.

This trip also included a drive to the Chapel of the Holy Cross which is built into the red rocks of Sedona. Another amazing place that is spiritual as well as healing. My sister Lori took a picture of the Chapel from the road and amazingly enough she captured an angel with its wings spread. How fortunate to have a picture like that.

None of us Bastien girls could go to Sedona the following year, but I did get my friend Kim to go with Donna. I knew that she wanted to go so badly but wanted to go with someone else. Kim has told me that she kept busy on this trip. She was very well liked and everyone wanted to spend time with her. This year she couldn't walk up the mountain. I heard it was mentioned to Maria and Jane who of course walked with her up a much smaller hill behind the Casita rooms behind the resort as far as Donna could go. This is now the spot that is called Donna's Mountain. I don't know the conversation that was said while the three of them walked but I do know that it had to have been special. I cannot thank Maria and Jane enough for having this experience with her and that they took the time to do this for and with her.

After Donna passed, Janice and I went to Sedona, and we took that walk-up Donna's Mountain with Jane and Maria. It was very touching to be there where she once stood. Jane had a reading that she shared with us.

Donna was featured in the 2012 Gloria Gemma Calendar, Her and Jenn, her daughter, were the January models and in her profile it said that she survived stage IV lung cancer and stage IV breast cancer simultaneously. Her miraculous recovery has taught her to live life to the fullest. She inspires all who meet her. This is an absolutely true statement.

Maria had asked her dear friend Wendy to meet with Donna and my mother who were going out to California if she would give them a tour of the San Diego Zoo which is where Wendy worked. They got a behind-the-scenes tour. Wendy had commented to me that it was a nice fun day and how she thought Donna was a gentle soul. She also told me how Donna commented with excitement about all of the animals and even how beautiful the plants and trees were. After the tour, she wanted to get a picture of themselves so she walked up to a man and said "you look like you need something to do" to which he replied "what can I do for you." She asked if he would take their picture. Wendy said that Donna made her feel good to be with her. It was always the same effect my sister had on everyone. It was beautiful.

Over the next year or so it appeared that Donna was going to outlast the beastly disease. Her hair had grown back which was good for her because she liked to look pretty all of the time. She had it styled so nicely, and she was wearing makeup again and dressing up as her old self. She enjoyed living free from cancer for a bit, not having to have any chemo or radiation. She still spent most of her time with our mother or the girls from the Foundation. She made so many friends there and they all adored her. I had met her a couple of times at one of her friends' houses where they all would eat pot brownies and laugh about nothing really. I loved seeing her like this, having so much deserved fun with these women.

I vividly remember the time she went to the Cape with some of her friends. There was a storm out that way and I kept calling her to come home because I was worried. Every time I called, they would laugh at me and tell me they were fine. When she got home, she gave me a picture of her and her friend Chris down in the water holding onto a huge anchor with life vests on pretending they were being blown away. I guess it was kind of funny looking back on it. This was the weekend as well that she found a little seahorse on the beach and seahorses for Donna were born. It became her symbol and when I looked up on Google finding a seahorse and its meaning, it said the seahorse is a symbol of good fortune/charm and attribute of the sea, the seahorse is considered to be a symbol of strength and of good luck as well. They carry significance in patience, persistance, friendliness, and contentment to name a few. It seems ironic that Donna came across that seahorse on that day. She had all these significant traits and although she had been to hell and back it showed how her strength and determination pulled her through the darkest days.

It was in July 2012 she had a routine PET scan which showed the cancer was back and with a fury. It came back in her lungs and had spread to her liver and bones. It was another vivid day for me because I happened to be at Brigham and Women's Hospital that very day for another reason. Donna and I talked the night before and we agreed to have coffee before her appointment. We met and had breakfast and then we went our separate ways, and I told her to let me know how she made out.

Hours had gone by, and I was still there. My partner was getting bloodwork taken when I got the call from Donna who said she was still there and that the doctor would wait for me to come down to his office. So, there I was pushing a wheelchair like a mad woman down the halls to his office. Of course, it couldn't have been good news, I thought. It took a few minutes, but we arrived, and they called us right in.

The doctor was standing, and Donna and her friend Donna, who had taken her up to Boston that day, were sitting. He asked if I would sit as well. I did. He began talking very calmly about how her cancer had come back vigorously and the dreaded words of "there is nothing more" they could do. What did he just say? Did I hear this right? Nothing else? Donna was doing well, this can't be right. We sat in silence and I was numb as the tears just started rolling down my face. I looked her way but it was so painful to look at my sister knowing that time was no longer on her side.

After a few minutes, I left the office and went out into the hall to try and focus on what was just said. I couldn't stop crying and I couldn't wrap my head around it. She would have to tell her kids and our mother and stepdad and the rest of our family. It was probably fifteen minutes later she and her friend came out into the hall. We just hugged and cried. This was just insane; she was going to kick cancer's ass! Not the other way around.

We decided we would meet at a restaurant not far from her house in Lincoln and talk. We got a table outside because it was a really wonderful day otherwise. I'm not sure but I believe we just started ordering Sangria. At first none of us talked a lot but eventually questions just started popping out. How was she going to tell everyone? How did she feel? How long was it going to be? After a couple of hours of being at the restaurant we said goodbye for the day. She had a lot to think about.

Everything went so quickly; her health was deteriorating but she still had enough in her to take our mother to the funeral home to plan for her death. She planned everything by herself. The casket, the pallbearers, who would do the readings, what she would wear, even picked out her prayer cards. How incredible that she made this decision to do all of this. I'm sure because not only did she want to but she also didn't want to have Derek and Jenn, her kids, to have to worry about anything.

Hospice

July turned into August really fast. For a few weeks friends and family went over to visit her while she was still talking, walking, and laughing like she did so well. She was a true diva having all this attention that she loved so much. I remember going into her place and seeing that she was getting a pedicure and manicure from her chair. People adored her and would do anything for her. She had a good few weeks.

My sisters and I had a sleepover and had a blast. We wore her old wigs that she once needed, listened to music, ordered food, drank and laughed. It was like we were kids all over, but we knew this would be the last time this would happen. The next day she wanted to spend her day with our brothers for the same reason. She had a family friend take pictures of herself with her kids Derek and Jenn and her grandkids before it was too late. She was already on oxygen and looking very tired.

Very soon after, Donna was not doing well and before we knew it, Hospice care was needed. She had originally said that she wanted to die at home and didn't want people coming over just to stare at her. That was how she put it. We had a cousin who was in a home hospice, and she remembered that people would be in and out all day just looking at her. Donna didn't want that. She wanted people to know her as a happy, smiley, fun woman and have that image forever.

She was on a lot of pain meds and needed them all throughout the day. Even though my sisters and I were shown how to administer, and we tried desperately to keep up, but it was too much. She would never be alone throughout this time; we all had taken turns to be with her and stay over in case something happened or if she needed something. I remember I was sleeping on her couch, and I heard her get up, by herself, to go to the bathroom holding onto the walker. She utterly amazed me with her strength and determination.

August turned into September. I was at my own home doing things around the house when Jenn called me to say that she had just gotten to her mom's and she was getting ready to go to hospice. Wait, I thought she wanted to die at home. We were both surprised, so I got in my car and headed back to Donna's. My brother Paul was at the house with Jenn. Donna was in her bedroom. I went in to talk with her and she said she was ready to go and asked if I would ride with her in the ambulance. It felt to me that time was standing still at that moment. I don't know why I felt this but also it seemed that the ambulance was never going to get there. We were all kind of just being for the moment. My mother was told it was time. She lived right next door to Donna, so she was ready.

The ambulance arrived and the medics went in to get her ready for the ride. All of her neighbors were outside when we came out, they knew what this meant. Jenn and I got into the back with her and talked to her the whole time. She even thanked us for going with her on this terribly slow and quiet ride to the hospice. There were no sirens, it felt peaceful.

I kept looking out the back window at my mother and brother who were following us in his car. I kept wondering what my mother was thinking, knowing that she was going to lose her daughter. The drive wasn't that long. Honestly, I don't remember Donna being taken away but what I do remember was the last time I was ever going to talk to her was while we were in the back of that ambulance. I had no idea that the next time I saw her she would be "resting comfortably" in the bed. She would never say another word. I was crushed. I had no idea this was going to happen. WHY? There was still so much to talk about with her. It was so unfair!

After that, everything changed. Word was out because she had so many families and friends that just loved her. People kept coming to visit. At one point the room was so full of people you had to stand at the doorway because you couldn't get in. Gary was sitting on the floor right next to her bed. I could sense his love for my sister, he sat with her for an exceptionally long time. That always stuck out in my mind.

The days that followed were emotional for everyone involved. Nobody really knew what to say or how to act, we knew what was coming. People came and went every day, all day. There was extraordinarily little sleep understandably for anyone. September 19th arrived and after a long day of people visiting and saying their good-byes, me and my nieces stayed with her. It was late I know, and the nurses set us up in loungers. One on each side of her and the third at the foot of her bed. I held her right hand while Jenn held her left. We were sitting quietly; I just remember saying to myself that it was okay for her to leave even, though I didn't want her to. It was time. She was tired and she fought the greatest of fights. She was a champion until the end and kicked its ass as long and hard as she could.

September 19th turned into September 20th which was the day she died. The three of us were with her when she took her last breath. Jenn, Renee, and I all heard it and immediately agreed it was over. Jenn and I were still holding her hands when she quite literally took a very last breath, just a very peaceful breath and she was gone. A nurse came in and confirmed the inevitable. Me and my nieces left hospice to tell my mother. She had already felt it. Another Angel got her wings.

The Funeral

The calling hours were on Sunday from 5pm to 8pm. People came to pay their respects but not many of them left right away. The funeral home filled up quickly and stayed full right up till 8pm. It was very overwhelming to see how many people Donna touched throughout the years. Childhood friends and families came, Relatives, people all through her years were there. I don't remember much else about the wake other than it was a sad time and I couldn't stop crying. None of my family could stop crying, we just lost a daughter, sister, mother, and friend.

The funeral was the following day on Monday, September 24th. My entire family was back at the funeral home and again people just kept coming in to pay their respects. It was an exceptionally large crowd that stayed behind to be a part of the procession to the church. The time had come to drive to the church. As we drove up to the front of the church, I immediately saw the Pink Color Guards standing outside in two rows facing each other holding flowers overhead so we could walk under them as we walked in. It was an extremely nice tribute.

During the mass, we all had our responsibilities that were chosen for us by Donna but unfortunately, I could not fulfill mine. I was an emotional wreck and I regret that I couldn't do my reading. It was the Reading from Saint Paul to Timothy which says "I have fought the good fight, I have finished the race. I have kept the faith. From now on there is reserved for me the crown of righteousness, which the Lord, the righteous judge, will give me on that day, and not only to me but also to all who have longed for it to appear. I say it now because I can."

After mass was the burial. Again, not easy to get through. There were so many people who came. I remember the pink bus and the pink firetruck. It was extremely somber. The priest said a prayer, and everyone stood in silence for which seemed to be an eternity. Nobody wanted to make a move, we just stood. After a while one by one people had stepped up to either leave a flower or take one. It was our final goodbye.

The Healing Years

Right after Donna passed the process of healing started. Not before the anger and crying had taken over first. This was the unimaginable that had happened. It was hard to even look at people without crying for days and weeks. Not much talking was happening. It was too hard to get up every day and have to live my life. I know my entire family was feeling the same way, but we didn't talk about it.

For me, I knew I withdrew from so many people. I just didn't want to face them, and I didn't want memories to come back to me because it was too painful to relive. I wanted to be alone with my thoughts. It was a while before I started the healing process. I didn't want to take care of myself, I didn't want to find an outlet, I just wanted to be angry and sad.

We all go through death in our own way and for me it took time to come back from it. Jenn had started going to cross fit to deal and as a result she looks fabulous and keeps up with it even now. It took a while before I could see people associated with her, The Gloria Gemma people, being one. They were all so good to her and I know they missed her too. It felt good and still does to see Maria, Jane, Kerri and anyone else associated with the Foundation when I do see them.

Healing is a process we all go through our own way, but I do think when we start to feel better it is easier to talk about our loved ones after their passing. Now that I look back, the best way to get through trauma is to talk about your person. It feels great to honor them in this way. The feeling that people smile when they share their own stories about Donna always makes me feel good. I did end up going for counseling which was something I should have done right after I lost my sister. I started to feel less angry and more supportive of myself by getting out my feelings towards death and surviving without her. She will be missed always.

Keeping Donna Alive

It's been over 10 years since we lost her to cancer but again there wasn't a day that she did not fight and fight hard. Asking me to write my story is the best way I can keep her alive. It is an honor to keep her going. People who read this who knew her personally will think about her and smile or even laugh about something that she did or said. I remember right after Donna died a whole crowd of us met at the Foundation in Pawtucket to release balloons for her. That was a wonderful tribute to keep her soul alive. There have been Christmas trees in her name every year that people see and remember.

In 2011, before Water Fire at the Providence Place Mall, cancer survivors as well as their family and friends got together to watch a film that had been put together showing the year before. The very last shot in the film was Donna carrying her torch and in slow motion she turned around and looked right at the camera. I was frozen and proud at the same time and will never forget that image. She looked so beautiful and happy.

There are so many memories that we have in our minds of her over the years. She is always within each of us who got the opportunity to have known her throughout the years. I had a tattoo put on my arm in honor of my sister that is a seahorse. I think of her every day and anyone who will listen to me, I brag about the seahorse because it gives me the opportunity to talk about her.

Helping Others

In this entire process of going through death as most people have, to know how we feel and what we think during all of it. The hate, the swearing, the praying, and the begging. The loving is what each of us feels. We cannot bring back our loved ones, but we can continue to talk about them and feel for anyone else going through the process we have been through. Sometimes it could be just listening to what they have to say with no response needed.

When I found out my young tenant at my house, Mary, who lived upstairs with her husband was diagnosed with breast cancer, I was stunned. She was so healthy and ran almost every day. This was crazy. She has had her journey and I am happy to say that she is a survivor. When I told her about me getting to write my story, she told me that she felt like she knew Donna because of the stories I had told about her and these stories helped Mary moves through her own journey. I feel truly honored that Mary would say that to me because she is a young, strong woman who never gives up. I feel like talking about Donna is inspiring and am so happy that in a way I have helped Mary get through without even knowing it.

There are so many people around us who can help others get through. The Gloria Gemma Foundation has the best resources and the most gifted people who work to help anyone who wants it. I hope this book will help others who are going through their own pain and understand they are not alone. We all figure out in time that we can survive living without our loved ones. Keep their memories alive forever is a great place to start.

Donna was my sister and my everything to me. I would do anything for her. I wrote this story from my heart and how I remembered her life through my eyes. I tell my story because there are thousands of people living who share this same experience. I want to make sure Donna's story didn't get lost.

Donna Genereux

CHAPTER 6

From Mom to Guardian Angel

In Loving Memory of Susan Sara Cutler
February 15, 1958 – January 4, 1996

By Melissa Bouchard

It was cold and dreary on the morning of January 4, 1996. As I opened my eyes and looked all around my room, something felt different. I looked at my alarm clock and saw that it was past the time that I am normally woke up to start getting ready for school. I was unaware at the time but there was a delay for school due to the snowstorm that had finally ended. As I laid there and slowly tried to wake up, I started hearing voices in my house and tried to figure out who it was and why they were there. The sound of footprints started getting louder and I saw my grandma turn on the light in the bathroom across from my room. As I watched her go in and out so many thoughts ran through my head. Why is she here? Who else is here? What is going on? Am I going to school today?

As I was trying to make sense of all of this, I heard a voice telling someone on the phone the words that frightened me the most. He was telling them that my mom had passed away. How could this be true? I must be dreaming. When I wake up this will all just be a bad dream. I could feel the tears starting to develop and then fall down my cheeks. This couldn't be real. I'm just not ready to lose her is all I could think about. I heard someone coming down the hallway again so I tried really hard to pull myself together. Once again, my grandma went into the bathroom and closed the door. I knew I had to ask her, but I didn't exactly know how to do that. How do you ask if your mom is still alive or if she has passed away?

The doorknob started turning and I knew I had to quickly think of something to say. Once the door was open, all I could get out was *"Hi Grandma, am I going to school today?"* She turned on the hallway light and looked down the hall at whoever else was in the living room. As she turned to face me, I just knew what she was going to say. I started to cry uncontrollably. Thirteen days before my thirteenth birthday, I had lost my mom to cancer.

Growing up my mom was full of energy and was always involved in everything my brother and I did. She was a manager of D Manufacturing Jewelry Company which sold costume jewelry. I remember how special I felt when she would bring me to work with her especially when it was the jewelry show at the Biltmore Hotel in Providence. I felt like such a princess and all the vendors treated me that way when she would bring me from room to room to look at all the pretty merchandise that was being sold. I remember this one company asked me about tennis and after I told them I loved playing it at camp, they gave me a beautiful pin that said I love tennis.

My mom and I shared a love for jewelry and sometimes when she would have to work late, she would wake me up when she got home and show me some of the pretty pieces that she had brought home for us to wear. She also loved being a part of the PTO for our elementary school. I loved having her at all the events, especially the father/daughter dance and the mother/daughter fashion show.

My mom was involved with our synagogue. She loved being an active member. Growing up in a Jewish household, my brother and I attended Hebrew school three times a week and went to all the services during the high holidays. My mom was respected and adored by most of the people she met through the temple. She loved being a part of the congregation and loved helping with events that they threw, including bingo. I still remember when my brother and I would work at bingo with her, it was nice doing it as a family. After her passing and with a generous donation, her name was added to a plaque that hung from the wall to the left of the front entrance until they no longer occupied the building. It was such a beautiful piece of art that helped remember those who are no longer with us.

During the time that she was battling cancer, I was getting ready for my Bat Mitzvah. My mom was so excited and had the rabbi come to her hospital room many times so she could continue to coordinate all the details.

Unfortunately, she had passed away prior to my Bat Mitzvah date and even though she was not able to attend physically, I know that she was with me and looking over me from above. One of the traditions during a Bat Mitzvah is to light thirteen candles and dedicate each one to a family member, friend, or group of people. I don't think that there was a dry eye in the house while I was reading my dedication to her.

> "I know she's watching over me from heaven and will guide me to the right direction throughout my life. I know if she were here, she would be very proud of me. Over the past year, she has been in a lot of pain but when it came to giving both my brother and I a happy Hanukkah, she made the doctor let her go buy presents and come home to celebrate with her family. I know to her the most important thing was to make everybody happy, even though occasionally she gave some doctors a rough time. Sometimes, it even seemed like she knew more than the doctors. She was the sweetest and most non-selfish person I know. I would like for everybody to remember her as the kind of person who always tried to give more than she received. Would everyone stand and join me in a moment of silence while I place the 1st and last flag on the cake?"

Throughout that year I went to many Bar/Bat Mitzvahs, which was tough because it was a constant reminder that I didn't have my mom at mine, and I missed her so much. One of my close friends decided that she was going to stand with me at each one during the prayer called the mourners' kaddish, which meant the absolute world to me. I don't think she knows how truly comforting that was for me and how much it meant to me at that time.

One of my mom's passions was basketball, she was an avid Celtics and URI fan. Growing up, we had a golden lab who was named McHale after my mom's favorite player, Kevin McHale. Her passion for the game encouraged her to become a basketball coach at CLCF in Cranston which stood for Cranston League for Cranston Future. Female basketball coaches were unheard of back then and a lot of people tried to get in her way of becoming a coach and coaching a boys' basketball team. While she was coaching the team, she never let any of the parents sway her decision on how she coached them. It didn't matter if you were the star player, if you weren't doing what you were supposed to then she would put you on the bench during the game. I always looked up to how she stood her ground and didn't let anyone bully her out of doing what she loved to do. My daughter takes after my mom in so many ways and is now starting to show a love for basketball.

My mom was always the life of the party, and I will never forget how much my friends adored her and loved being around her. It was very important to my mom that I always felt comfortable going to her for anything. I remember this one time that both my parents weren't crazy about one of my friends but told me I needed to make the decision for myself whether I was going to continue my friendship with her or not. Once when I was on the phone with this friend, and she had asked me to sleep over, since I was starting to see my parents' point of view, I had decided that I didn't want to sleep over at her house. I walked down the hallway to the kitchen where my mom was and kept the phone to my ear so she could hear my conversation with my mom. While I was asking her for permission, I was shaking my head no so my friend could hear her saying that I couldn't sleep over instead of her thinking it was me that didn't want to.

One of my favorite memories with her and my friends is the Friday night parties she used to let me throw. In her mind, she would rather us be at the house where she knows where we are and knows that we are safe rather than just dropping us off somewhere to hang out. Everyone enjoyed her cooking, and she would make us a bunch of yummy food to snack on including nachos which we all fought over. If at any point during the party I couldn't find one of my friends, all I had to do was go upstairs and there they would be, hanging out with my mom.

As the years go by, I can feel myself forgetting some memories and some of the details get blurred. I don't remember the date or even what season it was, but I remember like it was yesterday the day that my parents had broken the news to us about her diagnosis. My parents had gathered my grandma, grandpa, step-grandpa, aunt, and uncle together at my grandma's house so they could let everyone know. My grandma's house was a beautiful ranch located in Cranston near Garden City Center. When you entered the front door, the living room was to your left, followed by the formal dining room. There was a door frame near the dining room that had a sliding door which was always kept open except for this one day. My aunt and uncle had brought my baby cousin who was around one year old with them. My mom completely adored him and was so happy to become an aunt. I will never forget her trying to get him to say aunty by repeating it three times every time she would say it. My brother and I were responsible for keeping him company as the grownups gathered in the other room with the sliding door closed.

I remember thinking it was weird that the door was closed, but I never could have imagined the conversation that was going on at that point. I had no clue that they were letting the family know that my mom had recently been diagnosed with cancer and that she was entering a fight for her life. A life that was so precious to all of us. When it came time to tell my brother and I, they decided to bring both of us into my bedroom and sat us down on my bed. I don't remember the words that they used, I just remember feeling completely lost and wishing this was all just a dream. From that point on, my life was never going to be the same. My mom had felt a lump on her neck and instead of getting it looked at right away, pushed it off for a while.

Cancer treatments have changed a lot since my mom was diagnosed in the 90's. Unfortunately, they didn't have set treatment plans like they do today, nor did they have the pre and post chemotherapy medications that really help with the side effects. I remember peeking in my mom's room to check on her and seeing her scratch so much that it made her skin bleed. She always seemed to be in so much pain and so uncomfortable. It wasn't until my diagnosis that I began to understand all the different feelings she may have had during that time. After losing her hair, she tried wigs and hats to hide her baldness, but the wigs were very itchy, and she didn't really like wearing them.

One night we went to a buffet restaurant, and it happened to be a little windy in the parking lot. I remember the four of us walking to the entrance from our car and a gust of wind came and forced her hat to fly off her head. She was so upset and probably embarrassed that she wasn't covered up anymore. I felt so bad and wished so much that I could make this all disappear for her and make her all better.

Losing my mom at such a young age was so hard. I had to go through so many milestones without her which was so tough, especially seeing all my friends with their moms. My mom was my everything, she was my best friend. She came up with the idea that we both needed second holes in our ears, however my dad was not a fan and was against the idea. Instead of siding with him, she brought me to the mall and had us both get our second holes together. I don't really remember what my dad's reaction was but I will always remember how special it made me feel to share that with her.

Every summer, my brother and I would go to overnight camp for two months and we absolutely loved it. My mom had a routine in the morning which included going to Don's restaurant before it even opened and hung out with all the waitresses. During the summer while we were at camp, she would also take that time to write us a letter because it was important to her for us to get a letter every day, even the first day. If you have ever been to overnight camp, you know how cool you feel when the mail person comes around and they have something addressed to you. My mom was very well known at Don's restaurant, and they all adored her and treated her and the rest of my family like family.

I remember on Wednesdays my mom would pick up my best friend that lived two houses down and would bring us for breakfast there before bringing us to school. We loved those mornings! She would buy us scratchy tickets and let us order hot chocolate and anything we wanted to eat. It was our special time with her that we really treasured and looked forward to. After my mom passed away, a few of the waitresses from Don's came to check on us and even brought food to our house. It meant so much to us that they took the time to do this. Unfortunately, Don's closed down before my best friend and I had our kids so we never got to bring them there, but I love telling my daughter all about it.

This year my best friend and I met for breakfast at one of the local restaurants near us with my daughter and her son. In honor of my mom who was like a second mom to her, I bought the kids scratchy tickets to do at the table. They enjoyed scratching them and we loved having a moment with our kids like my mom used to have with us.

Hanukkah was one of my favorite holidays growing up. My parents used to have all eight gifts wrapped and out in the open for us to see. They had one rule, you either open one a night or you can open them all the first night. I remember always wanting to do one a night but changing my mind quickly after opening the first gift. We always dedicated one of the nights to celebrate with family which we usually did at our house. My mom would cook a delicious meal and then we would head downstairs and sit in a circle. When lighting the menorah, I remember my dad always played his keyboard which made doing the prayers way more fun. Once we were done, we passed out all the gifts and went around opening one at a time. I carried most of these traditions once I moved out and lived in my own apartment.

My mom was staying in the hospital during our last holiday season with her. I remember she made the doctors let her leave so she could go buy us gifts because it was important to her for us to not miss out. It's crazy how I don't remember everything she bought that day, but I do remember she got me a plain black winter hat. She wasn't fit to drive and was pulled over before she could make it home. My mom of course knew the police officers and after explaining to her that someone called stating she was driving funny, they escorted her home so they knew she would get home safe.

My memory isn't that great when it comes to the day before my mom passed away. I remember it was a big snowstorm and my parents' best friends, who I also called Aunt and Uncle, took us sledding. It was a great distraction for what was waiting for us once we got home. Cold, wet, and tired my brother and I came home after a long, fun morning of sledding. For those few hours we were able to be kids and not have to deal with grownup situations. When we entered the front door, we immediately heard screaming and crying coming from my parents room down the hall. In order to not be in the way, I ran to my room and sat on my bed. I didn't know it at the time but my mom's cancer had spread and she wasn't able to eat, sit, or lay down without being in a lot of pain. I could feel the tightness inside me taking over and I felt so alone. I didn't want to admit to myself that this could be the last time that I saw my mom alive.

Once the ambulance got there, they quickly brought the stretcher into my parents' room. Once I saw it pass my door, I ran out to the kitchen which was across from the front door. A minute later, they were rushing my mom down the hall and towards the front door. I remember yelling "I love you Mom!" however, I don't actually know if that was out loud or just in my mind. Seeing my mom in that much pain is something I will truly never forget. It was one of the scariest moments in my life. I remember feeling so helpless and being upset that I wasn't allowed to go to the hospital with them. How could I not be there with my mom? How could they do this to me? I had no way of understanding at that time why they made me stay back and why it wasn't right for me at twelve years old to be there with them.

My aunt and uncle took us back to their house until my dad came and picked us up to bring us home for bedtime. I was so mad that my grandma got to stay with her and here I was helpless at home. It's only now as an adult that I realize that they really did make the best choice at that time. There was no way that I would have been able to handle seeing my mom slip away. I also understand now why it was my grandma who stayed, it was because my mom needed her mom by her side. She of course loved us very much but I know for that moment she just needed her mom. I used to feel like I never got to truly say goodbye but I've realized that she is always with me and there really isn't a need to say goodbye. I know now after becoming a mom that you never question the love your child has for you, even when they are giving you the hardest time. I know that my mom knew how much I loved her and still do and how much she meant to me.

It is tradition in the Jewish religion that during the state of mourning, immediate family will keep their mirrors covered. For some reason, I had it set in my mind that I had to have my hair a certain way for the funeral and insisted for them to let me use the mirrors. I think it was just the only thing I felt like I had control of at that time. It gave me comfort when nothing else did. Most of that day was a blur, however I will never forget how large the funeral was and how many people were still trying to come in as we were leaving. The rabbi delivered a beautiful service and I don't think there was a dry eye in the whole synagogue.

Driving in the limo over to the cemetery, I remember being quiet and still feeling like it wasn't real. There was snow all around and you could see your breath in the air every time you breathed. Once everyone had found a place to stand, they escorted us out of the limo and into the seats in front of the burial spot. This was the first time that I felt like the wind was really her, showing me that she was there for me. I sat in silence as I listened to the service and let myself feel the wind surround me and give me a hug. She was definitely there with me and watching over all of us while one by one everyone took a turn throwing dirt on the casket. In the Jewish tradition, you always start by turning the shovel upside down and then can turn it the correct way for the rest of the time you are throwing dirt into the grave.

After the funeral, we went to my grandmother and step grandfather's house to sit shivah while friends and family members came in and out to pay their respects. We were at their house twice a day for a week while we were in mourning and sitting shivah. One of my favorite Jewish traditions that we did was on the last day of mourning. Our rabbi came by to lead us in a prayer and then took us for a walk around the block to symbolize us ending our time of mourning and to initiate the start of a new beginning, a life without my mom.

My brother and I were very different in the way we handled our emotions in regard to losing our mother. There were times that I distanced myself from everyone around me and felt comfort in being in my room alone, away from everything that reminded me of my mom. I really believe that the thing that has helped me the most over the years is keeping her memory alive and visiting her grave. I made a tradition for myself and was able to keep it going for many years. Every birthday and anniversary of her passing, I bring a dozen roses and place them all around her gravestone. I always break one off at the stem and place it over the O in mom. In recent years, I've been able to bring my daughter and have her help me place the roses on the grave. It's not the same thing as bringing her to see her in person, but it gives me comfort knowing that she knows who her grandma is and can still have a connection with her. After my mom passed, my dad gave me her wedding band which I have worn every day since and look forward to one day passing down to my daughter.

When you think about your wedding day, you think about how your dad will walk you down the aisle and your mom will help plan and get you ready for the big day. Not having my mom for this was very emotional for me. I know that she would have had so much fun planning and going away to the Dominican Republic where we had our ceremony. The main color for my wedding was my favorite color, purple. The reason I fell so in love with the color is because it's the color of my mom's birthstone.

The biggest thing I wanted for my wedding was to walk down the aisle on the beach barefoot, looking out into the beautiful crystal blue ocean with the sounds of the waves crashing all around me. I also wanted a way to represent my mom since she wasn't there physically. I found a small silver picture frame and asked the florist to put it in the handle of my bouquet.

Since I choose one that needed a thin plastic handle, it wasn't possible to attach it. Thankfully, the florist asked if they could figure it out on their own which I am so glad I agreed to. The moment my flowers entered the room, it had us all tearing up. In the middle of my beautiful white roses cascading down was the picture of my mom. It was everything I wanted and then some. I not only had my dad walking me down the aisle but now I also had my mom. She made sure to show me many signs that she was there, starting with that moment.

While finishing getting ready, my wedding coordinator came in to inform me that they see some storm clouds coming through but weren't 100% sure that it was going to actually rain. I had a very difficult choice to make, either risk it and have the possibility of getting married in the rain or have them move it to a covered area not on the beach. I was so torn since all I wanted was to be barefoot on the beach. My mother-in-law looked at me and said, we didn't come all the way down here just to watch you get married inside and we aren't afraid of getting wet in the rain. It was exactly the advice that I know my mom would have said to me. Once again, my mom showed up and I know she had a hand in moving those clouds right along so they didn't mess up my big day.

A year after being married, I became pregnant with my daughter. Leading up to my appointment where we learned the sex of the baby, I would have bet a million dollars it was a boy. Before leaving the house, my husband and I said goodbye to our cat and let him know that we were going to find out that we were having a boy. Once we were in the room, she asked us right away if we wanted to know the sex or if we were having it be a surprise. I naturally said we want to know because there is no way I could ever wait that long to find out. She started doing the ultrasound and paused for a moment to tell us the sex. As she is telling us, all I can think is yup we are having a boy but that's not the words that she spoke. Instead, she told us that we were having a girl and all I could say is, *are you sure?* Once I got it together and fully took in what she said, I instantly smiled. I didn't smile because we finally knew what we were having or because it was a girl instead of a boy, I smiled because I knew that was all my mom.

The special bond my mother and I had just had to carry on. She knew that I needed to have a little daughter of my own. To honor her memory, we named her Isabelle Sara after my mom Susan Sara. I love talking to my daughter about my mom and all the memories that I remember about her. It is very important to me for her to know who her grandma was and why she was so special. I will be very honest, my daughter looks nothing like me and I joke that I was just her surrogate for nine months but her personality reminds me so much of my mom.

In the year 2020, while most people were mostly thinking about Covid-19, I was also living my biggest fear. July 21st was like any normal day, I worked and took my lunch break to go to my routine OBGYN appointment. During the appointment, my doctor mentioned that my breast felt dense but that was very normal and nothing to worry about. I have been seeing this doctor since I gave birth to my daughter four years prior. I left that appointment feeling relieved and happy that I didn't need to return again until the following year.

At the end of August, my husband scared me and pointed out a lump that he had felt at the bottom of my left breast. My stomach dropped as I went to feel what he was pointing out. He was right, it was a large lump that felt hard. I had to calm myself down and remind myself that my best friend had just gone through the same thing only hers ended up being nothing.

Since I was scared to know what the lump really was, I tried to forget about it and pushed it off for a few weeks. After getting my period, my lump started bothering me and making me more nervous. At this point, you could see the lump bulging out when you lifted my breast. Instead of pushing it off, I messaged my doctor's office. After describing what it felt like and how large it seemed, they got me in on the Friday of that week. My doctor has a mellow tone to her voice that instantly puts you at ease as she talks to you. She agreed that it was probably nothing to worry about and that it's normal for things to hurt more during your period. Her calm, mellow voice instantly went away once she started feeling the lump that was causing me pain. Her voice that is normally so calming had suddenly changed to a stern tone and I knew that this was something more than nothing. She insisted that I wait while she called every lab to get me in for an ultrasound and mammogram. When I tried to tell her that I had to work and couldn't take more time off, she told me that this was a time that my health needs to come first and that I was going to get these tests done.

I left the appointment feeling so overwhelmed and began to bawl my eyes out. I called my husband and asked him to drive me to Providence because I didn't want to do this alone. Once in the parking lot, he had to stay in the car and wait for me because of the new covid rules. Afraid and alone, I went to get my tests done. My mammogram was first which didn't give the answers that we needed so they moved me over to the ultrasound room. The woman was very nice who was doing it and tried her best to distract me from all the thoughts that were going through my brain. After she was done, instead of telling me I could get up and get dressed, she told me to sit still while she gets the doctor to come take a look. This is never a good sign. The doctor came in and confirmed that this was indeed a tumor that is very concerning and said I needed a biopsy. Trying to keep it together as best as I could, I made the appointment for October 1st, which is the first day of breast cancer awareness month.

The weekend leading up to the biopsy, my family and best friend tried to keep me as busy as possible, but I was terrified and couldn't really think of anything else. One of my biggest fears in life was getting cancer and going through what my mom went through. While I was walking up to my appointment on October 1st, I realized that my mom was sending me a sign. It was her way of gently telling me that this was going to be cancer. On October 7th, my biggest fear was confirmed, and I was diagnosed with triple negative breast cancer. Not only was I scared to go through what my mom went through, but I was also terrified of my daughter going through what I went through.

After meeting with my surgeon and finding out more about my diagnosis and treatment plan, it was time to tell my daughter. I honestly didn't know how I was going to get through it and how was I going to stay strong for my then five-year-old daughter. My mom was by my side that day and she gave me the strength I needed to deliver this awful news to her. I remembered things that made it really hard for me when I was little and going through the same thing. I explained to her that the stuff my doctors took out to make sure I was okay showed that I was actually pretty sick. I told her that I had an amazing team of doctors, and that their main goal is to make sure that I'm still here to bug you to clean your toys. I will have to take a super-hero medicine that will help make me better but that I may be very tired at times. I told her that because of this she will get to have more playdates which will be really fun. I also told her that it will take my hair away so daddy won't be the only bald one in the house. As the words were coming out of my mouth, I couldn't believe how strong I felt and how motivated I was to beat this instead of being scared of it. As a mom, you want to protect your children from all of the bad in the world and at that moment I knew I needed to fight not just for me but more for her.

During chemo, I had playdates set up for her on all of my bad days. I didn't want her to only see the good sides, but I also wanted her to see that even though things are hard for me that everything was going to be okay. On my good days, I tried to keep life as normal as possible, so she didn't feel like she was missing out because she was the child of a cancer patient. Life was different enough with Covid, she didn't need to miss out on more just because I was sick. Instead of thinking back at this time as dark and depressing, I wanted her to have fun memories with it. My daughter's favorite color at the time happened to be pink so letting her know that the color that represents what mommy has is pink and that we would need to wear more pink clothes just made her day. Instead of making cancer scary, I made sure to be very open with her and celebrate it instead of hating it. I hope that when she's my age and looks back at my battle against breast cancer, she will remember the support team we had, the pink sisters we shared and the cancer that we kicked away.

Being involved with the Gloria Gemma Foundation has been incredible and I wish that there was a foundation like this around when my mom was battling cancer. She had a pretty amazing support system but there is nothing like having someone that truly knows what you are going through by your side. Every year at the Flames of Hope I submit my mom's picture in order to honor her life and to keep her memory alive. Sitting there during my first time attending as a survivor and seeing my mom's picture come up on the screen touched me so hard. During that time, they had a song playing that spoke about if there were visiting rooms in heaven and showed a daughter here on earth visiting her mom in heaven. As the song was ending you see the daughter walk over with her daughter which made me cry even more. It touched me so hard because it represented my life and brought it all to life for me. I do know that everything I went through was real but a part of me feels like it wasn't and at that moment I had no other choice but to be in the moment. It was the first time that I had really let the emotions out since getting diagnosed.

I have this idea in my head that my mom somehow found out that I was going to get cancer and ran down and yelled wait. She told whoever was responsible that if they were going to give me cancer, that it was going to be breast cancer. It's like she knew that this was a cancer that I could beat and one that would keep me here with my daughter. Growing up, I have always believed that everything happens for a reason and that you may not know that reason right away but eventually you would. Even after losing my mom to cancer and then later getting diagnosed myself, I still believe this to be true. I believe that having my mom as my guardian angel through so many life changes, including my journey with breast cancer, was her reason.

Losing my mom at such a young age was so hard and I felt so lost. I honestly didn't know how I would move past this and how I would be able to be happy again. Once the shock of all of it wore off, I made a decision to try to hold onto my memories of her as best I could. I learned that the more I talked about her and about our memories together, it truly helped me keep her alive. In the 90's we didn't have the kind of social media we do now, so I don't have all of the pictures and special moments captured and saved on social media platforms like others. Every year on her birthday, anniversary of her passing, and Mother's Day, I upload pictures of her and create a beautiful post to honor her memory. Doing this helps me feel like she will never be forgotten and that her memory will live on forever.

Talking about her and posting pictures also helps me remember all of the good and bad times we shared. Now that I have a daughter of my own, I love telling her all about her grandma Susan and how much I see her in her. What makes me so happy is that she not only loves hearing about her but she also really loves talking about her. I believe that doing all of this has really helped me in the healing process and has made me such a stronger person.

It is hard to lose a loved one at any age for different reasons. How we choose to deal with our emotions and healing is such a personal journey. One that we have total control of. I chose to become a stronger person and to be someone my mom would truly be proud of. Every day and every minute isn't easy but as the years go by, you learn how to redirect those emotions and how to celebrate the time you had with them instead of the time you have without them.

I know that for me, holding this all in would have led to a much different path. One that was not as rewarding. For those of you who are recently going through a tough loss, my hope is that after reading this you will feel some hope. Hope that at some point you too will find the reason for your loss and be able to find what traditions to comfort you to help keep the memory alive of your loved one. At the point you are feeling your saddest, try to remember that you are not alone. That you are stronger than the sadness that is consuming you and that one day you will be okay.

Susan Sara Cutler

CHAPTER 7

In Every Sense of the Word

*In Loving Memory of our Mom, our Nani,
our Family, our Teacher, our Friend
Elizabeth Cardona
May 26, 1965 – July 1, 2022*

By Sara Vazquez

Finding Out

It was the year 2014, I do not remember the words in detail, only that she had something important to share with us and it did not have the feel of something positive. What I do remember is the apprehension and that when she spoke it, the word cancer, the energy I felt from her was the fear of something final. What I felt in myself was not as fearful but more a problem that had to be solved. She informed us that abnormal bleeding led her to see a physician and they found a mass. The immediate recommendation was a full hysterectomy. She did not have much time to sit with it and that would be the first blow to her womanhood. She asked if we could accompany her to an appointment with her oncologist. This would be when she would be told of their findings and what options were available. It was determined that she had stage IIIc endometrial cancer, endometrial means that the cancer is spread beyond the uterus and cervix but not beyond the pelvis, stage IIIc meant that the cancer had spread to lymph nodes in the pelvis and or around the aorta. What we heard was that the odds were not in our favor. After the rundown of treatments, she felt that the most promising was chemotherapy, although she knew it would be no walk in the park. I think the only light moment of that meeting was that her oncologist looked like the straight-up doppelganger of Dan Ackroyd.

Hair We Go

In preparing herself for the effects of chemo, my mom decided she would invite some family and friends to a salon to join her in cutting her hair very short. I thought everyone who attended in support, and most of whom also cut their own hair, were incredible. When I envisioned how this would go, I thought I would shave my head in solidarity, and I couldn't do it. I cut it short, but I apologized and felt horrible that I could not bring myself to go any shorter. I thought about how much of my own femininity existed to me through my hair and knew that I was only feeling an ounce of what she was going through emotionally. I had a choice, she did not, although I do believe that was her way of taking back some control. Her hair would go but on her terms. She was mesmerizingly brave that day, there was such power in her poise. When she lost it all she did not like what she saw. She was deeply saddened, another part of her womanhood stripped from her. When in fact she didn't need any of it, that is when her soul shined through and for me, I couldn't see anything else.

Second Opinion

I will never forget the way this day made me feel, I went with my mom to an appointment at Dana Farber for a second opinion. She had a recurrence and was now considered metastatic. We wanted to check if there was more that could be done, and I think that part of us hoped to hear someone tell us there was some kind of advancement or new treatment that could be trialed. We were looking for anything that could give us more hope. She had sent all her records in advance, and we were waiting in the room together for the physician to come in and speak with us. She came in and sucked every bit of light from the room. It was not about the information she gave us; I am certain my mother was privy to it before we went. It was the way she told us, very matter of fact, cold and with absolute void of feeling and without what seemed, any knowledge of how human emotions work. In that moment, she could have very well been in a black robe and the female, human, physician form of the grim reaper. I had never experienced anything quite like it and I thought, I can't imagine that this is even her first time. Why would they continue to allow someone of that nature to be the person that delivers this delicate information? Essentially, she told us that my mother was going to die and that there was no reason to hope that it would turn out any differently. Cherry on top, the time would be limited. We knew this was a possibility but when someone tells you in such a fashion, it's hard to swallow. I could feel my mom and I trying to keep myself from feeling everything that flooded me in that moment because I knew what she was feeling, and it remains one of the toughest things I have ever had to do. I felt absolutely crushed and I wanted to cry but at the time I felt that I had to hold it for her. That if I accepted defeat, what would be her reason to fight? I refused to let that take form, we left and went out to eat, and by the end of our meal I think we felt a bit lighter. There was no way someone was going to tell us how we were going to go down.

It Took and She Gave

Every time my mother had a recurrence it took from her physically; it was brutal to watch. One time, her neighbor called me. She was frantic, telling me that she could hear my mother screaming and she knew something had happened, but her door was locked. I remember getting there so quickly that I arrived just before the fire rescue. My mom had fallen and was in pain and could not get up. They had to remove her with a blanket because she was in too much pain to stand, she screamed the whole way out.

When we were in her hospital room she was wailing and asked the nurse to bring her something for the pain. Without much empathy, he told her they needed to wait for an X-ray to give her anything beyond NSAIDS. My sister and I tried to talk to her and take her mind off it until they brought her for an X-ray. I myself did not think it to be too serious, as I knew that my mother had a low threshold for pain. After the X-ray, the nurse seemed to show more empathy and allowed my mother something stronger for the pain.

This time the cancer was eating through the femur bone and the bone had broken right through. She later had surgery to replace the femur with the first metal replacement of its kind and would not be a fan of it when it came to travel, as it would always go off at the metal detector and she would have to explain. Don't get me wrong, she loved to tell a good story and that was of a battle scar but she would feel terrible about the time that it would consume.

Besides this, my mother had gone through chemotherapy, a couple lobectomies that resulted in most of her left lung being removed, had been put on oxygen for the remainder of time and another surgery to attempt to relieve pain and remained in relative pain thereafter. I would never question her threshold again.

¿Habla Español?

"I remember you being in college while we were in elementary school and never fully understanding how strenuous that must have been. It was one of my first memories of your strength and feeling proud that you were my mom. You did all of this and were a working model of how anything was possible for us. We would often be asked in life how we were Puerto Rican and could not speak Spanish."

The story always was that in your journey of becoming a teacher, you witnessed the hardships of the ESL students and the mom in you did not want to see us struggle in that way, so you taught us how to speak English before we started school. Yes everyone, Spanish was, in fact, our first language. I did wish at times that I was fluent in Spanish growing up but thinking about it now, it helped grow a relationship with my grandparents on both sides and provided humor. While we could understand most of what they said to us, a lot of what they received in return was broken Spanish, and developing a moderate level in deciphering the English language with, at times, the use of hieroglyphics. We did not like speaking with other fluent Spanish speakers because they would laugh when we spoke. My maternal grandparents were great at holding it in and correcting us. We would also try to teach them, and we always thought that my maternal grandmother did not know as much but we would find out when we would try to get something over her in English and she would respond in Spanish, letting us know that she had learned, like us, to understand more than she could speak.

Not On My Watch

I can say my mother was phenomenal at being present. I cannot remember many times throughout my entire life that she was not there. I had my first thought of possibly losing my mother in grade school. We were learning about the negative effects of smoking. I would come home after school and at the time, I would find her finishing up or the smell lingering. I remember telling her about everything that I learned, and she told me after that I was relentless and would be on top of her every single day until she quit. It was not the first time I was a tough cookie, when my appendix burst at five, my mom didn't realize that it was something that life threatening that was happening with me. I ended up getting to the hospital just in time where they were able to treat me, and I had to stay for a while following the procedure. They wanted me to attempt to urinate in a bed pan. For whatever reason I was not having it. I told them I would walk to the bathroom. They did not think it was a great idea and wondered if I would have enough strength. I was adamant about not needing any assistance. I do not know what came over me, but I did it, I walked over there like a five-year-old elderly woman, but I made it. I could feel my mom beaming.

Her

She was Proud. She was proud of her Puerto Rican heritage, she was proud of her femininity, she was proud of her family. She was proud of her rebirth. She was the wildflower, not meant to be prim and perfect or to be defined by the common perception of beauty. I loved this part of her, the level she reached. She was intelligent and did not speak about things without doing her own research and being versed. Yet, she had her adventurous side, her willingness to be open and learn new things. She had her spicy side and the side that had the ability to drive me crazy, but I absolutely adored her. I am still in awe of everything she had the power to achieve, all while keeping humble.

Every so often my mom would get away from her authentic self and let herself become worked up over menial notions. As I guess we all do from time to time. Sometimes, I think she wanted to belong, but I don't think it was ever in her true nature. She was in a league of her own or as I would tell her "On a different wavelength." I think her true purpose was served with those she lifted and those who shined their light, those who had the capacity to see "her" and appreciate her gift.

A Teacher in Every Way

There is no doubt to me that my mother was meant to be a teacher. It was a gift that came very naturally to her. She had the ability to command a room but there was a down-to-earth ease about her that people trusted. My understanding when I was young was that she was considered the cool teacher, I know now that it was the genuine concern that she had for her students that made them love her. It was taxing for her, to let that part of her life dissipate through her sickness. However, a teacher never truly stops, I found her continuing to learn and teach in different facets of her life and in times where she was not aware that she was doing it. She attracted people into her life this way, with her passion to see others succeed. She had many friends, and she was a person that wanted to see people as a whole and people that she loved, do well.

Power of Three

During our childhood, the original Charmed series came out. My mother, siblings and I were all hooked. My brother says that he is the one who started using the frequently used phrase "the power of three" and that our mom ran with it and made it hers. She most definitely did, and added layers. Thinking about it reminds me of their first spell. "The power of three will set us free." How I wish that we could use that spell to rid ourselves of the sadness, maybe, figuratively, it is. That is when we were officially dubbed the charmed ones, her power of three.

Nani

If we were able to have her consensus, I believe she would say that her greatest accomplishment was her role as Nani, it would hands-down be the opinion of her grandsons. This also came to her effortlessly; however, I am sure that her grand gestures would also help sway the votes. She loved every minute of their arrival and being an active part of helping and watching them grow. She always modeled the love of a mother to me in action and showed me just how deep one could dig. I will always hold a particular time very close to me. She was going through chemotherapy and her eldest grandson was having challenges in school and she swooped in. My mother, a real-life superhero, Our Wonder Woman. She immediately became an advocate for him and in turn taught me how to be one as well. I cannot put into words experiencing my mom going through that level of pain and having me schedule his meetings within a time frame where she would have enough strength to attend. The magnitude of this display of love, will always stay with me.

Her Three Loves

"With my three grandsons John, Elijah + Caeden is a blessing that is most precious to me. No amount of money or worldly possession mean more to me than my three boys. I love my 3 kids Carmen Rachael, Sara Melissa and Eddy Jr. My rays of sun that shine to my stars as the sun sets. I can't even imagine my life without my power of 3 times 2! How blessed am I? I have a beautiful extended family and friends that are now family. I have so much support around me, for me…. Rachael, Melissa and Eddy- I love you more than life itself and I am so proud and blessed to be your mother. I want you to always remember that I love you- Please tell my grandsons that they are my life- that I loved, that infinite love that permeates across realms and time periods. Please don't let them forget me. I know my grandsons are with the best, loving, capable hands." —*Elizabeth*

I remember my mom saying she did not think she could love anyone as much as she loved her children, before her grandchildren were born. She would gush at any opportunity. She was the one I would call to tell her about my children's achievements because she was the only other person that truly shared the same enthusiasm, I know this because if they were hurt or treated unfairly, she also shared the same concern. I worry that I will not fill them the way she did, that there will be a void left in my children. That I won't live up to the kind of mother that she was to me. I think of her when I am being tested as a parent. How she taught us and how she held herself. I recently had to advocate for John, and I felt her physical absence. She had some friends that helped, and I was grateful, but I was in a position where I had to take center stage and it felt intimidating. Did I do enough? I feel like I have lost the safety net for my sons and myself and the result is that I feel doubt and fear. She had a presence and a power that I hope grows in me.

Baila/Dance

Anyone who really knew my mom knew her passion for dancing. She would love to share a story about how, if she could sing, she would have been a triple threat. I can feel myself smiling. It was one of her outlets. While she would occasionally break out in song, she was more apt to break out in dance. She loved dancing! She loved that it came natural to my brother and later her grandsons. No one could stop her, unless you literally had to pull her off the dance floor. During her party for her first remission, she was in pure bliss watching Eddy and John burn up the floor and later at my sister's wedding she lit it up. My mother had gladly accepted the request to dance in the mother/son dance with her new son-in-law. My sister was the bell of the ball, but at that moment, during that song "Vivir Mi Vida" during that dance, my mom was the star. Her energy filled the room, and everyone felt it. Everyone knew that they were witnessing something special.

The Call

Hospitals, doctor's appointments, surgeries, they had all become a way of life, the obstacles had become routine, and that day was another day in the life. I was supposed to go see you and make sure everything was all settled for you at home after your biopsy and you were supposed to come over the next day to hang out in the backyard. I was almost home from work, and I was informed that the hospital wanted me to call them and to have my siblings on the line. I knew it wasn't good. All I hoped was that it wasn't the worst. I pulled over and they spoke the words that I never wanted to hear. You were no longer with me, and I could not fathom it. I felt removed from myself and I could hear myself screaming in a way that was completely foreign to me. I screamed and I cried, and I was barely breathing. How could this be? Why? No! You came back every time, Mom.

Power

I was told that I would have to live without a major organ, my heart. How am I supposed to do this? It does not make functioning sense. I did not invite this in, I did not entertain the thought. I thought it was within my power to keep you from this, I had come to believe that I had. But I'm beginning to understand that it was never meant to be my power. You filled me and left me with everything I would need to step into my own with constant reminders should I start to lose my way. I will say that when you parted, you took pieces of me with you, I often long to fill them and my heart is heavy. I know the emptiness will endure. I know that I will continue to find joy and love but, in the present, it does not surpass the sorrow. In the present, it does not exceed the desire to have you with me.

Whirlwind

What I never understood before it happened was how demanding it is to receive such a shock to your system and then have to produce, to get yourself together enough to quickly make arrangements. You are still trying to sort out what happened and then you are forced to delve right in, shattered heart and all. I remember not wanting to make any decisions without all three of us involved. I know in some situations that may have proved difficult and that if it had been pre-arranged it may have been easier but overall, now that some time has passed, I think we worked rather well together, all showcasing our different sets of skills. We did not realize everything it entailed, especially when you are trying to honor the life of an extraordinary human being in a week all while dealing with all the aftermaths.

In my mom's case, it was loaded. It gave me a different sense of empathy for those that have had to endure this before me or for any time I have heard about a loss following my own. What I found from the experience is that the most loving thing a person can give is a great story or some words to let you know how much your loved one meant to them. When you are in that position you know how deeply you loved the person but other people affirming your why is the most touching and beautiful.

Sisterhood

On her journey of fighting and healing, she discovered. She learned about different things that interested her or might aide her, and by doing so she became involved with several groups of women. My mom found these groups to be helpful to her and she would often invite me to participate in some of the activities. One of the groups was through the Gloria Gemma Foundation, I was worried about her being a part of the group, as it was a Metastatic group, and any loss was devastating to her. These women were her friends, and she knew their stories and it would follow with her contemplating her fate. I never knew what to say. I did not understand how this could be helpful to her, but she became connected to these other women through a common experience, that only these special women could relate to, and I did not begin to comprehend the scope of this until recently, the importance of having this specific kind of support. And I am grateful that she did. My mother had these friends and guidance that helped lift her through that time, and some of them spilled over to me. The connections she made were so powerful that some of her friends have been assisting me in ways that she would have and being light when things feel dark, and she helped influence a full circle moment for me when I experienced it among other groups. It is moving to receive this raw graciousness or what she considered them to be, earth angels.

The Charm

I have slowly gone through some of my mom's writing, and I found some explaining the meaning of all her tattoos. This was in reference to my charm:

> "a daffodil, the birth month of March and for my daughter Melissa. She has certainly been a rock and my quarterback coach, sometimes pushing me more than I thought I could possibly go. I am so proud of the daughter,

sister, mother and friend you've become. I see me in you and I hope that I have made you proud." —*Elizabeth*

Mom, although proud feels almost like an understatement, I have always been proud of you and I find tremendous pride in being my mother's daughter.

Humility

One of her greatest lessons was the example of humility. Even if it took her some time, she always came back to that space. She could learn to accept what something was trying to teach her and that was the innate goodness in her. It was not about perfection; it was about growth. I would call her most mornings on my way to work, sometimes I just wanted to vent and one time she surprised me and didn't have a response to something I shared. I wanted her opinion, as I valued it, and she simply said that she was trying to work on being a better listener because sometimes that is all that people need. She would be amazing like that, when she didn't even know. Then she called me one time and I was able to practice that with her too. I was on vacation and at that moment I was in an area of the beach water completely alone. She was having a moment and felt bad that she was calling me while I was away. I told her not to worry and that the timing worked out. I mostly listened and tried to offer some solace and by the end of our call I sensed that she felt better. Afterward, I wrote something very simple, I am now so very full of gratitude that I had the chance.

I am here now
And I am here forever
In another galaxy
In another lifetime
You are a part of my fiber
And I will never let go
I will always find my way to you
Because you are a part of my being
And I will never stop
Until all of my pieces are home

Where have I been?

Unfamiliar to myself. I know the grieving process looks different for everyone but for me, I am not sure where I am with it. I feel like without even trying I have had to shift my focus to other situations or problems, to more immediate needs, to upholding an image to my children, to being whole enough to help others even at the risk of doing a disservice to myself. Some of the most trying occurrences have been my older son struggling and sharing how he feels that he lost one of the only people that truly understood him and my younger son having a hard time and feeling like a talk with Nani would have helped. All I could muster was that I felt the same.

I figured this year would be hard on all of us, experiencing all our firsts without her, there is an undeniable difference in the moments once filled with joy. I can say I have never had moments of happiness matched with an equal part of pain. I feel like I am a person who lost their compass and is now trying to figure out their way on their own. What I feel is that I must relearn how to live. I must learn how to live as a child without a mother. When I think of it all, that is what I feel like, an adult child. For me she was a constant from my earliest memories. She was an instrumental part of the better parts of me, of who I feel that I am, a part of my confidence, my identity. Without her I do not feel like my whole self. She was my backbone. Everyone is used to telling a person that is perceived as strong, that they have it. What is it that I have, composure? Everyone thinks I am strong when really, I do not have an alternative, some mornings involve not wanting to wake up because in doing so I will have to continue to accept the reality.

I keep going because if I allow myself to feel those emotions too deeply there is a likelihood that I will get wrapped up or just swallowed up whole in an abyss of darkness. I am afraid of that extent of unraveling. I keep telling myself that I must hold it together. I know I haven't been myself for just about a year and within it I have had moments where I feel invincible but also ones that do not require much to make me feel weak or small. Those I try to hide. There are times that I feel confident that I can speak about her and every so often I have to pause, but even with this interruption I have decided that I will never not say her name, if the time calls for it. I do not know if it was by design, but she made it nearly impossible to not remember her impact every day.

I love you and it seems like an impossible task for you to know it from my heart.

I can never be angry because you are everything, everywhere and I was blessed to have you.

I would never have it any other way even though it's hard to digest.

Every so often I try to understand why but I'm never mad, Mom.

I know you are where you are meant to be, creating in the great beyond, that we cannot even begin to be enlightened with.

I visit you, happy and without pain. Going wherever you are needed to display god's love and more importantly, his mercy. He chose an angel who could teach.

But it still hurts.

Every day I wish I could speak to you. I try to be strong, but I feel lost without you.

I want to speak to you so badly, I long for it to my core.

I'm not angry but I miss you, Mom, and I need you.

I will wait for you till the day I get to do the work with you.

He chose such a beautiful, dynamic soul and I couldn't be more proud.

I love you mom and I hope you can hear me and feel it.

I hope you can help heal the people that are broken, I hope that you can help heal me.

Knowing now what it feels like to be whole.

I love you mom, the way you loved me and the way I loved you.

I hear you.

She's Like the Wind

My mom loved Sedona. She started going on the women's retreat with Gloria Gemma about four years ago. She was so fond of it that on her second year going she invited my sister and I, and the following year I had the privilege of spending the time there mostly she and I. She felt the magic there and the presence of the Kachina mountain. It was her favorite. This year my siblings and I decided to leave rocks at the foot of Kachina in her honor. We did not pick the ideal time to climb up, no one else was really doing it and the weather was poor. Onward we went and found a spot. There was no one up there. We had just enough time to place them down before several gusts of wind started to blow at us. I half-jokingly said "Mom calm down, we know you are here!" We all agreed in laughter that it was her. Later I came back home and was in search of something else and I found this:

> "I have always been able to control the wind. I would always prove it to my friends growing up. Now, I always tell my grown-up friends and the ones that possess their own magic, totally get me. They have no doubt that I do in fact control the air in a way that would make it windy so that when we climbed my favorite tree in our backyard, that beautiful weeping willow in the center. I loved feeling the branches swaying left, right, front and back and then watching my friend's faces light up with awe because I did in fact ask the air to produce the winds necessary to give us that wonderful amusement type rides. You see back then we had to use our imaginations. I don't really remember too many trips to amusement parks in the early 70s.
>
> I just recently shared my ability to control the air to make it windy out with my grandsons. It was Halloween night and I was dressed as Wonder Woman and they were my superheroes sidekicks. I told them that I had asked the air to be windy for us so that we could feel its magic on such a beautiful night! And Presto WIND! I now ask my grandsons, "What is Nani's superpower?" I love when they answer, "Nani controls the winds!"—*Elizabeth*

Thank you for letting me know that you will be with me when I soar.

Sweet Dreams

I am still in the process of attempting to be still enough to pick up on my mother's presence, to see the signs that she sends. However, it has been clearer in my sleep. She reaches me in my dreams. I almost always know that I am in a dream and that I am being given the opportunity to share that I love and miss her but also to ask her questions. At first, I was not met with a response. Other times she has responded, where I swear that I will wake up and remember what she said, and I do not but I am okay with it because I know they had a positive aura and that I am not meant to have all the answers.

The clear messages that have been conveyed are that she will always be with me, she is happy where she is now and the last dream I had, she knew she would not make it and we still had a chance to live, and she told me to go. I was heartbroken but I ran, I looked back but because of her, I chose to live. My mom did not lay down her life in that manner, but she did not give up her hope in fear. I believe she wanted to nudge me and remind me that I still have a life to live and a purpose to fulfill.

Remember Me

"What I want future generations to know and in particular those of my bloodline, is to know how much I loved. How hard I loved and that I was happiest when I was being a kind, loving person, I want them to know that I gave of myself willingly and often times without expectation. I'm not going to lie, I'm far from perfect. However, I consider myself to be a pretty decent human being. I want future generations to know, that no matter how scared you are of what is not known, I always believed that being true to myself was the most loving, powerful gift that I gave myself, and ultimately them. I want them to know that I had so much faith in myself, and fellow beings of all realms, that I was able to put fear in its place. I realized that fear does not have a place in survival situations, however, too much fear can be crippling. I would have said that my greatest fear was dying of cancer, however, my biggest fear is of being replaced and finally forgotten." —*Elizabeth*

What is Love

"I have always known that there is no greater love, than self love and our ability to love, rests on our ability to love thyself. I have always known this, and I never doubted it, and this gift will never leave my side. I have always known that I was able to pass these gifts to my Original Power of Three, and I'm lovingly passing these gifts over to my Power of Three Squared. I have always known what I have always known. That I AM LOVE!!!"—*Elizabeth*

And so, it is.

Through this process, I have discovered that this is not a story of grief, this is a story of an abundant, profound, reciprocated, demonstrated love. My mom is love and love is eternal, and this is but a love letter of sorts, because of you mom, I could write a book.

Sara Vazquez & Elizabeth Cardona

CHAPTER 8

Wonder.

*In Loving Memory of My Queen, Elizabeth Cardona
May 26, 1965 – July 1, 2022*

By Eduardo Vazquez Jr.

Wonder. It's all I seem to do lately, but not in the same way that she did it. She was brilliant! One of a kind, and she knew it. Yet even in everything she embodied, there were still so many things that were wondrous to her. For her life was captivating, but for me, I feel captured. Stagnancy and darkness have become my neighbors, but they won't become my home. I know that I won't feel like a resident here forever, but sometimes I wonder when I'll feel out from under. I wonder when this lease will be up. When will a room be held by my own light again? I wonder when my inner strength will match the pictures on these walls that I portray. When will my smile return and be as infectious as hers was and make this house a home again?

For now, her essence is the momentum that drives me. It's the only thing that cancels out the negative headspace that I have worn like a helmet. Except, this helmet doesn't feel like it's protecting me. Instead, I feel like it's encroaching on any hope I have of ever truly processing. I know that there is no such thing as love without the absence of it. Like many things in this world, we are meant to feel the moments of existence and the moments of absence. I know that grief is a part of feeling as though you've lost that love. I know that I feel lost because my love misses hers. It's searching for hers. But what I don't know is that I've even begun to grieve.

I wonder where one starts. I find myself desperately wishing to be at a place where my feet are under me holding me up again with purpose, but have I done anything to get there? Standing upright is what I've been accepting as enough. The only thing I find myself doing consistently is struggling. I've not shared much with anyone. I can barely speak about her without caving and writing seems to be that much more challenging. Encouraging my mind, body, and soul into working together harmoniously isn't what it used to be. Even back then, they weren't entirely bonded, but now it's as if they've completely fallen out. It's as if they're fleeting, but I know it's time to gently command their attention. In doing so, I hope that I can find genuine peace, where I once held it.

I know this is just a fraction of what I truly need and where my journey of healing begins. It begins with reminders that at times ricochet off one another beautifully and other times where it may feel like nothing is happening at all. I'm keeping in mind that every day is allowed to be as different or just as similar as the one before. The hope remains the same, and the hope is that one day my heart is feeling more full. I heard a song the other day that said something along the lines of, "my love it's just a reminder, find your center." I immediately felt compelled to share this with my sisters. It resonated with me and seemed like a good place to start. Her love is a reminder that I can find my center. It's a reminder that I can heal.

Even though every day is another day without her here as we know it to be physically, she left a legacy so full. She left a catalog that has provided me with nourishment, when I have felt at my weakest. It is her love letter to the world and one that I've come to realize she is still writing. I often think that it's a letter that now we can continue writing together. Sometimes the reminders come in many and others just a stand-alone reminder. Either way, they're forever there. Ingrained in my memories, my thoughts, and my feelings are precious little gifts that at times are very subtle and at times crystal clear. It's almost as if she carefully selects them to be as such. I feel constantly surrounded, as if she is at an arm's reach; even if that arm can no longer grab ahold of me like it used to. Having given herself fully, she created a vast space for me to bask in. I've come to appreciate that this is part of what makes up a legacy.

While the pain is unbearable, I am so proud of her. There are not enough words to really explain all of the ways. Beyond that, I am so fortunate. She is a love that comes in many forms now, even though the lack of the physical form is the most evident and one that I miss immensely. Grasping onto the forms she left behind, I pay attention to what she is sharing with me. She is teaching me, from the other side, that both the pain and the joy of this world need to be felt. She is reaching me in capacities that are familiar, and many that are new.

    I stand on these grounds we once walked on together, and I feel these familiarities, most of which are in our very own backyard. She loved mother nature and all of her elements. In all of her glory, nature proved to be monumental for her. From some of her nearer favorites like the willow tree to lilies, I see her waving hello, I'm here. In some of her more distant favorites like the red mountains, I see her standing tall and with great strength. She led me to Sedona this past year, and what an experience it was. It was easy to see why she loved it there. I was told she walked through the red sands and kept any trace of it that it left on her shoes, so I followed in her footsteps. Later keeping the remnants as they instantly became sacred to me. I took photos where she once did, one of which was in front of a set of butterfly wings. It was my way of saying Mom, I made it. But I already could feel that she knew. I felt overwhelmed with joy and sadness. I couldn't tell which was winning. I often imagined myself with her and my sisters, all there together. I guess we finally were. We climbed the mountains and left painted rocks in the most perfect location in her honor. I hope and pray they are protected, as they lie in a space within her favorite mountain.

    Apart from the visual phenomena that is the red mountains, I got to experience the spiritual feeling of the vortexes. They really encapsulate you in a medley of inspiration, restoration, healing, and awakening. All of which she already embodied but sought more of. I felt her blanketing me the way they did and telling me that it's time to wake up from the momentary slumber I had allowed myself to fall into. I felt awake. I felt her presence strongly in the winds, a couple of times when capturing a moment through a lens. While the wind doesn't show in the exposure, I'll always know that in that moment, she joined in. Each breeze feeling more and more intentional caused a shift in me. They felt more special. They feel more special. It's sort of like that gentle back rub someone will give you, without saying a word but also saying so much. A touch can really speak volumes that way. I understood them, and took them as guidance and protection. Prior to this experience, I had recently read a passage she wrote saying how the wind was her superpower, which speaks to how I appreciate it now. My superhero, I feel you loud and clear. The way the winds move me and touch my skin is her way of letting me know she is present. It reminds me of her might and strength but also her coolness and ease.

Although I can never share a touch as we did before, I happily welcome them as they are now. That's not to say I don't feel the connections she can make. I feel her now in the connections I share with others in a similar embrace. I feel her in the kisses and hugs I receive, while never taking a single one for granted. At times I try my best to hold for just a little bit longer hoping that she feels it too. I know this may come across as unusual, but sometimes I hold my own hand when I need that physicality, because my touch is her touch. My flesh is her flesh. My sight is her sight. My voice is her voice. My step is her step. My dreams are her dreams.

I dream of her often and when I open my eyes, I see her at every corner of this world. That is how connected she was with life and with a love of pursuing it. I see her in every hue of green. She loved color altogether, but emerald was her absolute favorite. I see her in every butterfly fluttering weightlessly through time and space. I see her in the symmetry of their wings and the gracefulness of their demeanor. I see her in the mystery of an owl's expression. I see her in their intent. I see her in the way they guard their surroundings so fiercely. I see her standing tall like a lighthouse serving as they do, as a beacon of light. I see her in distinct patterns, and eclectic designs. I see her in a freshly painted manicure. I see her in jewelry of a similar aesthetic to hers. I see her in art. I see her in the many women who march to a similar drum and those who march to the beat of their own. I see her in those who are proud of their culture. I see her in anyone who is unapologetically bold. I see glimpses of her in them, and I see her in glimpses within myself. I take all of these in as affirmations that she wants me to push forward. I often re-imagine how she would encourage me to lift myself up and how my happiness was her happiness.

I'd give anything to actually hear her voice again. To hear her say "I love you sweetie" or "this is my baby" which was always accompanied by a kiss, when introducing me to anyone. I miss her voice tremendously. I still hear it vividly. I enjoyed her distinct way of speaking then, and I enjoy it as I hear it now. I find myself playing videos or messages just to hear her laugh. I loved her laugh. It was so contagious, voluminous, and unique. It was the kind of laugh that drew yours out. She had a tone and a frequency all her own. It was one that she'd all together laugh, sing, and speak with. Part of what made her voice so intriguing to me wasn't just its sound, it was how she used it. She spoke with purpose and understanding. She spoke a language of love with passion, pride, conviction, but also a gentleness. Sometimes I echo those moments to myself, whenever I doubt exactly what my journey is from here on out. Songs play and instantly they take me to her. I can hear her celebrating and singing along. She was the life of the party, raising her voice when something was particularly her favorite part or when she had something to say.

She was a force. It's one of the reasons nostalgia has become one of my favorite places to frequent. Remembering feels good to my soul. They say it's best not to live in the past. I agree to a certain extent, but I will gladly visit her there every single day. They were the best times of my life, and for that I am blessed. Out of all of the possibilities in this world, my path didn't just cross or align with hers. I got to be her son, and she will always be my mom! She will always be present and I know that's where she would want me to start. So I will. She is still loving me and still carrying me. Even now, she is saving me. Her name is Elizabeth, and I'll forever say her name.

She was a powerful woman, just like her name exuded. A warrior queen, whose tribe was always inclusive and it indeed included many. It's how she's always been, a woman of the people. I was always so impressed with how many people she knew and how intricately she described her relationships with them. No detail was left unturned. You could always feel the significance whenever she'd share how she crossed paths with them. Rushing to share what made someone special or unique.

I was raised by a remarkable woman, but before that she was a remarkable little girl. Growing up I remember her sharing stories of her childhood. She would share stories at every chance. While most of them escape me, I remember how much joy it brought her. It was just wholesome. She loved her parents, siblings, and her friends. She showed me photographs, many of which my mom kept sacred till this day. She valued keepsakes. They served as testaments to where she came from and who and what she valued. She always told me how fortunate she was to have a strong foundation. No matter what happened, whether it be good, bad, times of struggle or pure fun, family was everything to her! That included those she chose as my family too. There were hardships of course, like any upbringing but she always faced adversity with her head and her heart. I can speak to that. I can't speak much to her childhood as it was before my time but I know she was lovely. How I wish I could go back in time to see little Elizabeth growing up. She was beautiful, intelligent, eccentric, charismatic, loving, and adventurous. Every bit of that, I got from her.

We were the wild ones, and I wouldn't have it any other way. Being loud, proud, and comfortable in our skin was just in our nature. Sure, even the best of us have our days, but if we were left of center or outside of the box, we were perfectly fine with that. I realized this during my own childhood, into my adult life. It was this strong yet unspoken bond we shared that would only evolve with time. We never tried to tame each other. I don't think we could even do so if we tried. We basked in what made us, us. Whether it was an introverted characteristic or that of an extrovert, it didn't matter. You were being you, and we loved to relish in it. She would defend my inner spirit like no one else would. I think she knew that you could be an adult, but still enjoy spontaneity like an uninhibited child would. Even as adults, we continued doing the very same.

As I write this, I smile thinking how if I ever forgot, my mother would always take every opportunity to remind me and the world for that matter. "You get it from your Momma" she would always say, or "Don't hate me 'cause I'm beautiful!" I loved her tenacity. She had a grip on things but wasn't afraid to let go. She showed me that you can "throw caution to the wind" yet remain grounded and human. My mom was proof that there was room for both, never being defined by one side of a spectrum. There was always room where you made it. There was always space for improving and excelling too. If you had a desire to achieve a goal or chase your passion, she encouraged you to pull the full weight of yourself into your own corner. You weren't there alone though. She was there too, because it was who she was. She was a teacher, the unsung heroes of the world. It was one of her divine gifts and something that came so naturally to her. When I was much younger, I'd go to class with her and spend time with her students. She was the cool teacher. She held her ground but also showed her students she came from similar roots. More importantly than that, she truly wanted them to succeed and grow!

I've had several talks with some of her students back then and some when they paid their respects. My heart beat through my chest when one of her former students said "Your mom being my teacher saved my life." She left her impact. I think if you can even reach or save one person's life in your own lifetime, you are fulfilled. But before she was a teacher, she was a student, a friend, and a mentor. She was the cheerleader in your corner before she became the captain of the team. Either way you looked at it, she was a teammate through and through. She remained humble and in her eyes, you were parallel.

I feel more fortunate now than ever to have met her on that level, as an equal. Although she led by example, you weren't following her. You were side by side and that we were. Growing up, I had my share of insecurities. Some might find that hard to believe because of how loud of a personality I am at times. It's something my mother would always push me to continue doing, but she was also gentle with my quiet side. I appreciated art. I loved drawing and dancing as a child. While the drawing was something I held more privately, the dancing she and I shared together. From watching her dance in the living room at gatherings to dancing at my sister's wedding, she was electrifying! I was so proud that night to see my mother move the way she did. It was fascinating! She danced with her soul. It was as if she was pulling from all of her ancestors who came before her. If there was a dance floor, she was on it! If there wasn't one, she made one! If her favorite song was playing, she was dancing. Her arms were out grabbing yours for a dance before you even knew it. She was that kind of woman. My mother was a proud Puerto Rican Latina in the way that she moved in life and on the dance floor. She even had a few signature moves that I'll forever only know to be hers.

I definitely got some of my swag from her. From watching me dance as a child, to dancing as a young adult, she showed up and showed out. I'll always remember one moment, when I was on stage ready to perform. There was a delay in the music and the crowd was relatively quiet. It was probably a twenty second delay that to me felt like hours. My body was trembling, and at first, I only heard soft voices of encouragement. But not if my mother had anything to do with it. I remember hearing her shout "I love you! That's my boy!" which filled up the room but also soothed my nerves. It didn't just calm me, but I can honestly say I felt how proud she was that I was her son up there. I felt pure joy right then and there. From the moment that music started, I felt charged. She supported me, and any form of art I was passionate about, one of which being the art of drag.

I loved sharing that passion with her, because I love it as deeply as she has loved her arts. It's one of my fondest memories with her, that night that I performed in drag. I could see in her eyes that she was intrigued and in awe. She was a true believer but more importantly, she was my rock. She never wavered on that. I often think about the next time I perform, when I'm on stage, the lights are beaming, and the music starts filling the room. It all together breaks me and puts the pieces back together knowing that instead of being in the audience, she'll be right with me on stage. It'll be a moment when we dance together again, and I look forward to it. It's hard looking forward to things, but I can honestly say that will be a moment full of joy. I know she'll once again help me get my spark back.

From the most recent times back to my childhood, I was marveled by her. I loved that connection we had of being brave, artistic, and free. I love that she took every opportunity to express her love in a way that made me feel it. That's where the beauty lies. I was not the average boy of the household, but I was still growing into the man of it, in her eyes. She allowed me to grow and even though it took me quite some time, I finally got closer and closer to my truth. She gave me the space and the time that I needed. And through the entire journey, I always felt safe with my Mom. When I came out to my mother and told her I was gay, I remember how still she was. She was so poised, but very attentive. She was listening to me, and I mean actually listening to me. Unfazed and unbothered, she simply said okay. Telling me she loved me no matter what was something I felt in my soul. It went without saying.

What I found to be the most endearing was the comfort I felt in the things she did not say. What I mean by that is she didn't have some generic response or pretend to know anything. She didn't say "I knew." This moment wasn't about validation. It was about vulnerability. She didn't need to say anything more than what she wanted me to feel. What I felt in that moment, to date the strongest that I've ever felt, was unconditional love. That is the very moment that I understood what those words truly meant, fully with every fiber of my being. She saw me, and she loved me unconditionally. I'll always be grateful for that moment, because for me it was only once in my lifetime. And I couldn't have asked for a better way. It allowed our relationship to reach even newer heights and it opened up the doors for more learning and loving. Countless memories we captured through a lens or in the stories we'd tell, but none would do that moment any justice. It was the feeling.

Becoming an adult alongside my mother was probably my favorite part. There's nothing quite like that bond you share with someone after you've learned some of life and what it takes. I will always be her baby and her third born but I got to be the man she was proud of too. I am the last to complete her "Power of Three," which is how she referred to my siblings and me. It was a phrase she used but even more so, it stood for the deep love she had for each of us. My two sisters and myself all had our own bonds with her but we were unified in being her rock. It is the most beautiful thing when the person you adore the most adores you the very same way unequivocally. I sit and think what an honor it was to be thought of that way by her. Not just because she is my mother but because she engulfed herself in the extraordinary.

Later on, my three nephews would be born, and they became an extension of that. For her we were her greater loves, followed by them, her greatest loves. Sometimes I wonder how she had that much love in her. No words could ever capture or convey what I could spend the rest of my life trying to say, but I hope this does it some justice. My heart clings onto one thing the most, when the days just don't feel the same, and that is that I know she loves me and she knows I love her. No matter where we are in this world, we will always exist. It's something we created that can never be duplicated. It's something we share which together, we made everlasting. No amount of time or distance can alter it, for it is divinity at its finest. It's powerful. It's how the "Power of Three" came to be. You see love wasn't just one entity for my mother. It was layers and layers and generations of love multiplied. The more she loved, the more she had to give, and I'm entirely grateful to be one part of that equation.

At one point I felt that I created a slight divide in our equation, when I moved across the country. I don't mean just a physical divide, but in part, an emotional one. Leaving everything I knew was one of the toughest yet most necessary decisions I've ever made. I remember how sad she was to see me go, but I also remember her telling me she knew that I needed this new adventure. There was a deep understanding that this decision was vital.

My mother always resonated with a quote my grandmother used to say, and it was "la vida es para los valientes". This means "life is for the brave". She would say this often, and I remember her saying it to me during that time. In that moment when I was leaving, I knew I needed to be brave for her too. I was the fearless one, but both of us were crying on the inside. Smiling through tears, we both knew how pivotal that moment was. She always told me to live my truth and that required bravery. The truth is, it was hard leaving that love, but I needed to live a life that I was proud of. The only way to do that was to live an authentic one. In this case, living my authentic life in part meant that I needed to find it. Starting somewhere new was the first step in a very unknown direction.

She continued to protect me, but she was still very careful with me. I think she did so to ensure she didn't alter the path I was on. She wanted me to decide when to turn or if I'd turn back. She didn't want my journey to be influenced by any fear or doubt. Sometimes life can be like that. Someone says one thing and it changes your trajectory. I know she didn't want to be that person. I'll always admire her for that. As a mother, I can't imagine how difficult it must have been to choose when or when not to say something at such a delicate time. I do however remember her telling me that she never wanted me to water down who I was anymore. She told me I had spent too many years doing that, and ultimately she just wanted me to be happy. It took moving away for me to finally do that. It felt like I had come up for air after being underwater for so long. Sure I was swimming through life, but when was I going to come up for air to breathe? While it made her sad to see me go, she was the sole reason that I could even do what I did to begin with. It pains me to think that the one person who shaped me was also the one person I made the saddest. Anyway you look at it though, she is why I was brave enough. She was my reason!

Eventually, certain things came to light and while I know it was hard for her, she had to take down that blanket of protection in order to be honest with me. At times she would tell me only what I needed to know and nothing more. But the time came when only transparency would do. It was a very hard conversation when she told me that she had cancer. I remember exactly where I was, and how my stomach dropped. I didn't want to do anything but go to her, but she insisted I stay on my path and carry on. You often hear stories but when it happens to you, it shakes you to your core. Every single thought imaginable crossed my mind. Everything I thought I knew felt erased. I felt unhinged, but just like my mother always did, she helped me center myself. It's a wild thing to be comforted by someone who's going through the actual painful part. I felt horrible for that. Even through her pain, she brought me solace when I needed it. She brought me peace. There was no storm, because she surrounded me with calmness before it ever was cast.

For a time, I felt guilty. I felt terrible for not being close to home. She would ask me if I would ever move back, but she never truly asked me to do it for her. Part of me wishes she did. I'll always live with this feeling that I should have moved back. Guilt is one of the most horrible feelings, especially because it starts from within and eats away at you. I thought I knew what it felt like but truth is, I didn't until now.

The saving grace is that my sisters were there for her every step of the way. I will spend the rest of my life being grateful to them for that. I can't even express the lengths to which my sisters went because I wasn't there, but I should have been. My mother would always reassure me that she fully supported me living far from home. She would tell me that my happiness was enough, and I believed her. There's just some part of me that will always feel guilty for not rushing to my mother's side the moment I found out. Even when this feeling hits the hardest, I feel a sheer lightness in my heart knowing that she would tell me that she forgives me but there is no reason for me to even feel this way.

Even still, I watched her fight for years. She didn't just fight, she all the while celebrated her life. She all but put her troubles on the back burner and hardly ever let them show. She was a survivor and later on she became a sister with her new pack, joining Gloria Gemma. She shared her experiences for a greater good, and she didn't let it change her course. She was driven. Even when it took a little bit of her every time, I watched her do the unthinkable. She would go on to replace what she may have lost physically and replace it with something new spiritually, each and every time. It took, and she replenished. Those voids were filled with forms of new and existing love, and new and existing passions. When I thought I couldn't be more impressed with her, she impressed me at every turn. I wonder how she did it. Elizabeth underwent a rebirth!

She began writing again, traveling more, learning new things, accomplishing new goals, finding new passions, and dreaming again. She'd probably humbly give credit elsewhere, but she herself breathed new life into the one she already had. It was magical! She was as fierce and proud as ever. She was unstoppable. She became a woman of wonder and to see her flourish anew was unworldly. She was our "Wonder Woman".

My world then changed when I received a call from my sisters. It was a conversation that I was told needed to include all three of us. My heart sank. My body felt crippled. I didn't want to believe what was about to be said to me, but I knew it was coming. I was praying that I was wrong. I desperately wanted to be wrong. I sat down hoping I wouldn't hear the words, but then I did. I can't even write them down. A part of my soul had gone. I could not speak. Hearing my sisters on the line crushed me. I couldn't bring myself to say anything to help them. I could not move. Even the act of thinking was far too taxing, but my mind raced wild. My mom had bounced back every time. I didn't think this time would be any different.

I can't even begin to explain how I was feeling. This was not my reality. It didn't feel real. I suddenly felt hollow and the bits and pieces of me that were still intact just felt numb. I guess feeling numb was better than actually feeling in that moment, because the only thing I'd have felt was pain.

Days passed where I did absolutely nothing, and every single thought I had somehow found its way back to her. She deserved better is all I kept thinking every time I thought of her. And I kept reliving that moment over and over again. It was damaging. I felt absolutely helpless in my own thoughts and in my own body. I wanted out of myself. I didn't know if I wanted to be alone, or with someone else. I was grateful though to have friends by my side. It's almost as if that part, being the only, was meant to be. Something about not actually being alone during that moment spoke to me. But I still had no idea how to really receive any kind of love or condolences. I was broken, and now it just feels as if the tissues have scarred but the damage still remains.

I was in a very dark place, imagining if I'd be better off not being here anymore either. I hated thinking that way but the mind is a powerful thing, when it's filled with sadness and despair. I know this isn't what she'd want for me, but it was hard convincing myself otherwise. I know I wasn't alone here and while my sisters and I shared the deepest pain we'd ever felt, my mom is what held us close. She'd want us to stay together and keep going. I started looking at pictures of us all. Seeing her moving and laughing kept me afloat.

At night, I'd often dream about her, and I'd take it as my new reality with her. There we get to exist too. I'd tell her I love her, and she'd tell me she loved me too. Some dreams, she'd look at me and no words needed to be said. I felt everything she was telling me. She is still here, and even there in my dreams, her energy is just as infectious as it had always been. Being asleep and dreaming often felt better than being awake. But each time I'd wake up from a dream with her, I'd feel just a little bit stronger and a little bit wiser.

Embarking on new adventures where she once was helps fill me and carry me. If it is one thing about Elizabeth, it is that she is going to make her presence known. She'd never take no for an answer, and she'd never leave our side. But still I struggled to grasp what my life is like now. People would say how strong I am, which is something that I got from her. But I don't feel strong at all. Songs would play and I'd just cry. I wanted to smile and reminisce, but my heart was battling between joy and pain. That's the thing about pain, it hurts but it reminds you of how deeply you loved.

Every day I try to lean into the moments but just when I do, I'm at war with myself again. Will I ever feel that magnitude of love again? Will anyone ever love me the way that my mother did? I wondered. Will I ever embody all of the characteristics she was once proud of? Will I ever just be me again? These are questions that I know I'll find the answer to, but how?

From this point on, it won't be easy. I've realized that this void will never be filled. How do you fill something that was once occupied by something that was one of a kind? When I think to myself, I try to not focus on filling that void but more to supporting it. Surrounding it entirely with the one thing she embodied the most, love. Finding my way back, finding my footing again seems more possible this way. I think this is the only way I'll be able to move again the way I once did.

Curling into a ball seems more like my current state of being, but I want to run through the fields again where I know she'll meet me with a gust of wind. I want to be able to scream her name from a mountain top, or even softly amongst those I feel safe with. I don't know what it is but I feel blocked. I can't really speak about her with others. I've not been able to write or express myself when it comes to her. I've not been able to share much. I feel trapped in this new home. I've not felt safe. What am I standing on now, because what I've known to be my foundation for my entire life is not here. There's a part of me telling me I need to build my own foundation, but how? Leaning into everything that I still love seems to be the obvious answer but moving in that direction just feels impossible.

My sister once told me something along the lines that all of the beautiful things in life are often scary at first. So I did something that took me completely out of my comfort zone. I had recently taken a trip overseas completely on my own. What I found by doing this was that some new life had found its way back to me. It was almost like I was starting from square one, but with the support of those back home. I've done this before. I faced new challenges the same way she would. I opened my heart and was ready to accept whatever love and embrace came my way. After the nerves left, I felt excited. I felt like one of the people. I felt safe. I explored a new city and took the culture in. And to my surprise, I was taken under the wing of several new beautiful people that I now called friends.

There was a part of me that completely submerged myself into something that felt divine. Not having done this in a while, I felt reborn. It was exactly how it was supposed to be and exactly where I was supposed to be. It dawned on me then, that this was the first time in a long time that I felt at home. I know there is no exact answer to all of my questions. I know that everyone's path of healing is different. But for me, I think my path starts with rebuilding whatever makes me feel at home, after a love lost. Taking what I have now and combining it with the new. It's what I did during this new adventure. Realizing this early on during my quest was a gift. A gift that I know within my heart of hearts came from her, my mom.

A day came where I felt her presence so strongly. It was as if she was whispering in my ear all day, to let go. I was surrounded by the greatest love I've ever known. The time was now to take my first step. I needed to face what I once turned a blind eye to. This was my chance of coming out of the abyss. This is something she did time and time again. There was no reason I couldn't do it here and now. So I took off running through the fields, in a foreign country, as the sun was setting, with people who were new to me but felt familiar. The wind caressing me as I ran served as a voice of reason. And I was listening. Knowing and feeling she was with me in a place we'd never been was blissful. But now, it is a place we fully embraced together and one where I felt some healing. It's a new connection we share, just in a different way from how we would have before. It's still just as beautiful and serene as any other memory we cherished. It'll forever hold a place in my heart. It proves to me that I can heal and reaffirms that our love will always exist in the here and now. So now when I wonder, I'll do my very best to do it the way Elizabeth did, because my mom is brilliant. She is love!

To myself:

Eddy, your life has changed as you know it, but that doesn't mean that there isn't any beauty left. Try not to be so hard on yourself and if you slip, get back up. Healing can happen and will happen every single day. For some people, you're that constant reminder of love and light. For some people, you bring them joy and laughter. So, hold on. You are your mom in part, because you came from her. Your love will always exist, in one world and all the others. Be happy, because you deserve it. Love yourself, because now loving yourself also means loving your mom. Your Momma is with you always!

To Mom:

I'll spend the rest of my life being eternally grateful, and I will wholeheartedly continue to receive your love in all the ways you continue to share it with me. My love for you knows no end. I've said it before and I'll say it again, out of all of the possibilities in this world, my path didn't just cross or align with yours. I got to be your son. Thank you for being my mom! I miss you.

"The way that you are loved is immeasurable.
The way that you embodied that love is treasurable.
The way that you metamorphosed into love is remarkable.
The way you left a mark, is timeless, where no clock could go"
—*Eduardo Vazquez Jr.*

Rest in eternal power, my Queen. I love you.

Eduardo Vazquez Jr. & Elizabeth Cardona

CHAPTER 9

Not Yet, Mom

In Loving Memory of Joanna King
February 17, 1956 – August 6, 2020

By Jeanette Simoes

Mom's Story

Mom was beautiful, magical, funny, smart, sassy, and sophisticated. She always had her hair curled, a bit of makeup and red lipstick. In my childhood, I could always remember her getting ready for work. The smell of her Estée Lauder perfume was everything. It had this sweet rose smell to it, to me it was her signature smell. I always loved her uniform, her navy-blue skirt suit with her red and white Delta Airline scarf. She was a Senior Delta Airline ticket agent at TF Green Airport. She was there for thirty-five years before retiring. I believe she would have stayed there longer; she had a bad back after her first pregnancy, it just got worse over the years.

In her earlier years with Delta, I remember she would bring me and my sister to the airport and take us to the back room where most of the Delta ticket agents would have their breaks. My sister and I would get excited, we knew there would be food. There always were bagels, breakfast sandwiches, fruits, and sweets. You name it, they had it. My mother was friendly to basically all her co-workers. She made lifetime friends with a few of them that we still see today. Those co-workers we grew up with and their families. We call them the Delta family. We are very blessed they are a part of our lives.

Mom was always a family person. Family was number one. If someone wasn't happy, she would find a way to make them happy. I loved that about her. On my mother's side her dad, my grandfather, was in the Navy. Then he retired, residing in Rhode Island with my grandmother. He became a chef at Rhode Island College. My grandfather was from New Orleans and my grandmother from Virginia. My dad's parents were from New York. Funny story, my grandmother on my mother's side was adopted by my dad's stepdad's parents. My dad's mom ended up being good friends with Mom's mother and that is how my parents met. My parents ended up being together for forty years. They had a fairytale love. Nothing was perfect, but they loved each other and their families. After my parents got married, they moved to New Orleans for a little bit, then they decided to raise their family in Rhode Island. My mom's parents had a huge backyard. They talked to the city to see if they could build their home on the property. The city approved it; they were able to build their forever home. My mother was so excited to start her life in Rhode Island close to her family,

My mother had a sister and a stepbrother. My grandfather was married once before he met my grandmother, and they had a son together. My aunt lived five minutes away from us, and my uncle lived forty-five minutes away, closer to the beach in South Kingston. My aunt in her college years lived in New Orleans with her aunts while she was in school. My uncle's side of the family lived in Hyannis. He would visit there in his younger years; he stayed in Rhode Island, got married, and had three children. We were all a beautiful family. I love how we are all so close and had beautiful times when we visited each other.

One day on a family trip to the Bahamas, my aunt meets a Bahamian man, she dates him for a couple of years, and they ended up getting married. It was a beautiful wedding which was in the Bahamas so my uncle's family could attend. My aunt literally had seashells on her headband that attached to her veil, the colors of the wedding were black and white. The bridesmaid's dresses were so pretty with white fluffy shoulders and velvet black dresses. They were pretty for a late eighties dress. A couple of years later they had a little girl, we were all so excited! A new baby in the family. My mom's parents had a condo in the Bahamas, where they would go for the winters. It was so cool. If we ever wanted to go to the Bahamas, we would always have a place to stay. A home away from home with better weather. Those times were beautiful. After my aunt got married, her husband moved to Rhode Island with her. He was a good cook and became a chef in Rhode Island. I would say our family had great perks between travel and food. We were living the life!

As the years went on my sister and I grew up, got married and had our own families. We were still close with our parents, and we always resided in Rhode Island. My sister had the first grandchild. My parents were so excited! Finally, a grandchild, and it was a girl. So, another princess to add to the family. My niece became so close with my mother, they were best friends. My niece helped my mother heal in so many ways. My mom always had issues with her back and had seven back surgeries. Every time my mom was sick, my niece would help take care of her. It was tough when mom got diagnosed with the cancer, it affected everyone. I know it affected my niece in a different way.

Through the years with the family, we had our ups and downs. My aunt unfortunately got divorced sixteen years ago and moved to Georgia with my cousin and never looked back. We would still go visit her when we had the chance. My uncle in South Kingston got divorced years before my aunt did. He still resided in Rhode Island and so did his children. The family was sad, everyone was cordial with each other, things were still good.

In July of 2020, we got a devastating call, my aunt's daughter had undiagnosed Crohn's, and it was too late to treat. She ended up passing away. We were completely devastated; she was so young. My aunt was heartbroken. Her only child. My mother loved her niece as if she were her own. Our family was so sad, but we had to keep going and make sure our aunt was at ease. That was not easy. When my cousin passed, Covid was in rare form and we could not go and see her in Georgia. That put a strain on us, especially my mom because she was the type to go, no matter what. She was going to see you. Mom knew this time she could not. My mom at this time was already diagnosed with cancer for six years. It was a big risk for her to travel, any of us too. This was a very trying time for our family. We had to figure out a way to keep the family strong.

She Was Not Well

In mid-2016 I noticed when we were having a good time at one of my previous work events at Six Flags with the family, Mom kept holding a cold-water bottle on her chest because she said it was burning. She had been holding that water bottle to her chest for about a week before the event. We never thought anything of it because she always was sick with something. Before going to the work event, we told Mom to make a doctor's appointment because her pain was not going away.

A week later after the event she goes to the doctor, they take her back in that cold doctor's office to speak about her chest, take some notes, and do a cat scan. After the doctor's appointment, we were hoping for the best and hoping it was nothing serious. A couple of days later we get the call from the doctors. They say "Joanna, we see a mass in the back of your breast, near your sternum. You have cancer."

Sigh. The silence after the phone call was so scary. You could hear a pin drop. Mom did not know what to say or think, we were all speechless. We all took a day to process the phone call and then we all got together in the kitchen and said, "Let the fight begin".

Mom started her first treatment. I remember my dad, grandma, and mom going to her first treatment, the building was cold, but the nurses greeted us with warm hearts. They welcomed Mom with open arms and brought her to her big reclining chair that smelled like medicine and sugar cookies. I looked around at some other people getting treatments and I was sad. I was happy they were getting treatments and hopefully that nasty cancer gets out of them. It was time for mom's first treatment, the nurses hooked up the tubes and the IV bag to her port, Mom was in pain when they did that. I felt so bad, I held her hand and said, "this too shall pass and soon you will go home and rest."

After four hours of her first treatment, it was time to go home. she got up, a little wobbly, but she still smiled and was ready to go home. When we got home, my dad took her up to their bedroom, put her blanket over her, and she went to sleep. Dad stayed with her in the bed and rubbed her back, it was a sweet moment I captured in my heart. The love he had for Mom was priceless. I went home to rest. The next day I checked on her, Dad said it was a rough night, the nausea medicine helped a lot and, overall, she is okay. I felt at ease. Mom became a pro after her first treatments, taking her meds, eating better, but she did not like her hair falling out, that was the one thing she could not stand. We all told her we loved it; she always rolled her eyes.

As time went on with treatments, Mom ended up getting a brain hemorrhage. Thank goodness my dad came home for lunch that day and checked on her. He ended up taking Mom to the hospital because she wasn't acting like herself. When they arrived to the hospital, the nurse asked her name and date of birth. She didn't know it. That's when they took her in the back right away and did a cat scan on her brain. While waiting on the results, they prepared us for the worst. The nurse said, "Sorry, she is not going to make it".

Her brain was swelling severely. My family's heart sank. We were lost. I said, "this cannot be it."

After waiting more hours finally, the neurosurgeon came in and spoke. "We can take the hemorrhage out safely and your mom will be okay." We could not believe it! She is going to live. My body felt like it came back to life. The neurosurgeon said, "it's time for surgery."

We waited again in the cold hospital with uncomfortable seats. As I was waiting, I rested my eyes. I thought I took a cat nap, but I ended up sleeping for an hour. My dad shrugged my shoulders and said, "your mom is out of surgery." After the surgery, it was a long process getting her back to herself and fighting the cancer. Mom had to learn how to walk, speak and even learn how to eat again. Once she healed and was well enough to take chemotherapy treatments, she fought hard and beat the cancer. Mom was in remission. She was our superhero! She had stage IV metastatic breast cancer from the start. The tumor was dead. Of course, she was checked regularly. We were excited that there were no more treatments.

In that time of remission. those few years were wonderful. I had my son in 2018, her first year in remission. My mother was ecstatic to have her first grandson, she said he will call me "YaYa" I thought the nickname was so precious. I couldn't't wait for her to just live her life with her family, and she did.

She traveled more with my dad and the family. They went to the Bahamas, Disney, Atlantic City, and visited family in Atlanta and we went out to eat more as a family. We were simply enjoying her presence. Mom never really healed 100% from her brain hemorrhage but she still had her beautiful smile and personality. We were all so happy she was still with us.

In late 2019, Mom started to feel achy and just not well. She called the doctor for an appointment; they did blood work and of course the cancer was back. It came back fierce! Mom did not want to give up. Not yet. She received more treatments and became sicker. Late September of 2020, after a treatment, she just could not bounce back. We took her to the hospital to receive fluids, we thought she would come home in a couple of days. Instead, she declined over the days, and she never left the hospital. I can remember the feeling I felt when I knew she was not leaving the hospital. The feeling of being lost in a crowd of people you do not know. In the crowd I wanted to find my mother. She was not there. It was such a scary feeling, I knew I had to find my way out of being lost so I could be there for her.

The Passing

The day before she passed, I was holding her hand and telling her it is okay to let go, not feel pain anymore, and to go be with her niece and her dad. I did not want her to go yet although I knew she had to. Those days of Mom declining were the hardest, knowing that she will not wake up and soon will not physically be with us anymore. We got the call, 3:25pm August 6, 2020, she had left to feel no more pain. I knew when my phone rang that was it. I did not want to pick up and I did not. instead, a text message. it said "3:25" with a heart emoji. I lost it. I cried and screamed and said "Why? Why my mom?!"

My friend of thirty plus years happened to drive by my parent's house to drop off dinner and she saw me crying in my car. She knew automatically that I had received the call. Her hug was everything. I calmed down, walked into the house to be with my sister, dad, and grandma and start to heal.

The days after mom's death seemed like years. You just know the final goodbye is coming. The day came. I looked at her lying in her casket. To me it was not her, it was her vessel, tired from the long fight she had had. I touched her hand and said "I will forever be kind and patient like you. Love you Momma."

The long day of tears and heartache finally ended; I was happy to get home, take off my shoes and unwind. As I was taking off my shoes I started to cry and realized she was never coming back. How can I live without her? I thought at that moment I could never live without her, but I'm doing it. A year after her passing my grandmother's dementia and Alzheimer began to decline. I have become my grandmother's caretaker, on top of taking care of my own household, my autistic son, and being a wife. I began to feel overwhelmed, drained and emotionally tired. As time went on, I realized I needed to take care of myself more and help myself heal with the grief of my mother's passing.

Starting Something New

A couple of years after my mother's passing, I decided to pursue some new things. I always wanted to learn how to play the violin and read music. I remember how scared I was to enroll in lessons. I kept saying to myself "Can I do this?" Well, I am doing it. I'm currently enrolled and taking lessons in violin and music theory. I never thought I would do something like this and it's wonderful. One day I hope to play a song dedicated to my mother. She loved music and loved to sing.

Another thing I decided to be part of is a grief counseling group with Gloria Gemma. I was skeptical at first because I didn't want to talk about my mom's death or how I was feeling about it. I knew doing that would put me in a sad place. I was wrong, it put me in a good place. Talking to the group and hearing the other stories of loss helps me heal a little better in my heart. I am so glad I decided to join. I've also learned from the grief group that it's okay to grieve when you want or how you want. Sometimes it's hard to walk around smiling knowing, deep inside your heart is broken because the person you love is physically gone forever. I've learned that it's okay, my heartache won't last forever. My mother will be in my heart forever.

Finding Peace

It took me a good couple of years to find peace in my mother's passing. I was very upset she died. I wanted her to be here with me and the family. She couldn't. How I dealt with this was to accept she was never coming back, and death is a part of life. Things I already knew, but I didn't think she would die so soon in my life. I thought I would have my mom for a very long time.

I started to heal from my hurt. Self-care, getting massages and facials are great things to get your mind off daily stresses. Self-love, I've learned to love myself more, love my hair, body and personality. It helps to motivate me every day to get up and go. I connect more with my friends, go out, and enjoying myself more.

My mother always enjoyed the life she had on earth no matter how much pain she was in. She kept going no matter what. I say to myself all the time "I will keep going no matter what". Truly those words will forever keep me going. I hope you will find healing every day and keep going. In time, you find comfort and joy in your heart.

Challenges and Change

Figuring out how to live without my mom is hard. I couldn't focus right. I was so used to her being around. I literally didn't know what to do, my panic attacks started to get worse, my personality was slightly changing. I felt as if I was becoming someone different and I didn't like it. Eventually as time went on, I started to get back to myself a little, adjusting to my mother not being in my life. I started to accept a life without her, being a mom, caretaker and a full-time worker. I was doing it all! It amazed me. The things I thought I couldn't do without her I was doing myself; my fear was tested, and I was passing the test. I was very proud of myself. It made me feel stronger and wiser. It made it a little easier to move on and live my life because I knew I could do it.

Before my mom passed, my mother-in-law died a year before. The pain of losing her took me over the edge, I loved her as if she was my own mother, finally I was at a place where I was okay living without my mother-in law. A year later my mother dies. I said to myself "Why would I lose the two most important woman in my life, so soon?" A question to which I would never get the answer, that is okay.

After a few months had gone by since my mother's passing, some challenges came along. My husband and I noticed our son's development was delayed. We had him tested. The doctor said, "your son has autism spectrum disorder." To hear those words were a blur at first, then it clicked in. I said, "okay, what are the next steps?" All I wanted to do was call my mom, cry and hear her comforting words. I was mad I couldn't call her. This new development was challenging. I never had anyone on my side of the family with autism. I wasn't sure how I was going to handle things going forward. I did what my mother would do, I went with the flow. My son is non-verbal, and he didn't pick up on sign language. I feared how I was going to communicate with him. His ABA program suggested a communication device. He picked up well on the device and I was so proud. I wish my mom was physically here to see him grow, I know she is here spiritually and that is a beautiful thing.

A year went by since my son's diagnosis, I needed my mom more than ever. I started to feel like I was a failure because my son was getting older, and his challenges were getting bigger. I was scared and so was my husband, we didn't understand why he was acting in a certain way. He was hitting his head and getting upset easily. With help and lots of meetings with specialists we were understanding autism more. As time went on my husband and I were struggling with everything, finances, communication, and not treating each other well. We were also grieving; we really didn't have a moment to sit there and talk about our grief. Losing both of our moms a year apart was difficult. I struggled with trying to find happiness in our marriage, it seemed like we were just living a routine life and not having any fun. Fun, the thing that always kept me going. What I was missing about my mother, was her fun. I wasn't getting enough of it. I started to communicate about what I needed and what he needed as well.

The happiness was quickly fading, and it was time to figure out how we were going to fix it. At the time all I wanted to hear was my mom's voice, saying it was okay. I had to deal with the changes and challenges we were going through, losing our mother's and other close family members, a son who had autism, and taking on being a caretaker. Our lives changed so drastically because we lost so many close family members in such a short amount of time. We didn't have time to sit there and grieve our loses or take time to ourselves to talk about our grief. This caused us to go into a downward spiral. Fighting was starting to become a normal thing. I told my husband we must do better for ourselves and for our son. We started to communicate and love one another again. It's not perfect although we got into a better place. We started to listen to each other, go out on dates, talk about our feelings, and what made us get to that point in our marriage. It was not easy, we had to keep it going for the both of us. It was challenging to do and still is. We are doing our best for our son and trying to love the best we can.

My Grandma Delores is my mother's mom. Before my grandmother developed dementia, my grandma and mom were always together traveling, shopping, and enjoying their grand kids. Grandma always had a sharp mind and never missed anything. It was hard for her to see my mom decline in her health. A year after mom passed, I noticed my grandmother's health started to decline. She had developed Alzheimer's/Dementia. Grandma had minor Dementia a few years prior to mom's passing but in time it had gotten worse. Luckily, before she started to get worse my grandmother graciously gifted the house to my husband and me. After getting settled in the house and a routine, I became my grandmother's caretaker, which is amazing and very exhausting at the same time.

Becoming a new mom, homeowner, and a caretaker I was very overwhelmed and exhausted. I needed my mother so badly to the point that it hurt. I had to get myself together for my family. In the beginning, taking care of my grandmother was tough! She didn't want to take her medicine, her mood was up and down, her eating was poor, and she was sad. My grandmother knew the one person she saw every day and took care of her was not coming back. I felt it was up to me to make her feel comfortable and get her smiling again. In time, my grandmother got into her new routine with me taking care of her every day. Some days are great, and others are not. All we can do is take it day by day and try to live a full happy life.

My dad was always a prince and my mother the princess. Losing his princess was difficult. My dad was always with my mother, cooking for her, cleaning, giving her medicine and just plain loving her. It was all taken away in the blink of an eye. My dad was trying to pick up the pieces of his broken heart. It literally was so sad to see my dad sometimes, he would just sit in his chair and just stare and would say "how did my life turn out this way'? His princess taught him to still run the castle without her and he is. My parents were the couple you looked up to. Their love was like no other. I always admired that. Always traveling, having fun, watching and laughing at their favorite shows, and most of all being with their families.

When Mom was diagnosed, my dad was always right by her side making sure she had everything she needed to get better. It was hard for him, deep inside when you know you don't have that much time left. When Mom went into remission for two years, Dad did everything possible to live a full, happy life with her. They did more traveling, enjoyed their grandkids together, and just loved each other a little more. It made me happy to see that but broke my heart knowing time was not a lot of what we had. Dad took us on a big Disney trip a year before Mom passed away. It really was one of Mom's favorite places to be and for us too. Being there, we knew inside that this was the last time. I hated the feeling knowing maybe this was her last trip with us. It was.

To see Dad and Mom having the best time was magical. Dad always made Mom feel magical. The day Mom went back to the hospital I could tell Dad had an uneasy feeling like maybe this was it. I told myself it will be fine, she will get fluids and recover and be okay. That was not the case. I called Dad from the hospital and said Mom was being admitted and not coming home just yet. Dad came right to the hospital and sat there. I could see the sadness in his face. Every doctor that came in had a different thing to tell us. "She will be fine" or "Your mom is really sick." We all looked at each other, like okay we know she is sick but is she coming home? An answer we would never get.

A couple of days went by, and Mom got worse and so did Dads' heartache. During Mom's last days it was Covid, and only one person every hour could go and see her, my sister was with Mom while Dad and I waited in the car for the next visit. I will never forget the call from my sister saying this might be Mom's last day. My father started to cry. I never see him cry. My heart sank to my feet. He knew his princess was not coming back to the castle. The next day Mom passed, and Dad cried some more, even though he was feeling sad, he made sure my sister and I were okay.

The days after Mom's passing seemed like we were all dragging along. Living a life without her was tremendously difficult in the beginning. The family was trying to figure out how all of us would live without her. Our family dynamic was being tested because my dad worked until 5pm, my sister worked and my niece was in school. Usually, my mother was the one to help us juggle our lives, because she didn't work. My mom was super helpful, taking care of my son and my niece. I usually pick up my son thinking that if my mother or mother-in-law had the kids I wouldn't have seen the kids until they went to college. That is how blessed we were.

After a couple of years passed, dad was exercising more, getting into shape and even cooking more! He was starting to move on, and it was okay. It was nice to see. It made me feel good knowing he is not completely broken inside. Dad always said, "I will always live my life for her" and that's what he is doing.

Her Legacy

Mom was a beautiful, fun soul on this earth. Her physical presence was everything, anyone who knew or got to meet her was lucky, wherever she went, her smile and personality would light up the room. Mom also enjoyed Broadway plays and casinos. She enjoyed the music of the plays and noises of the slot machines. The family enjoyed those as well. When my mother retired from Delta Airlines, she continued to work part time for Harrah's Casino. She would put people on flights to Harrah's Casino in Atlantic City. Of course, when she had the chance, she would go to Atlantic City. She literally would tell my dad a day or two before she wanted to go, he would say "to my goddess Joann! Tomorrow!" She would say "Well yes!" I always laughed because my dad would get mad, then he would say "let's go to Atlantic City." My dad always went with the flow, even if things didn't flow right.

My mom always enjoyed the life she lived. I believe it's why life with her was amazing. Nothing is perfect, I always enjoyed her. The thing that hurts the most for me is missing how she made me feel. The feeling of always being loved and happy. I am still a happy person, just my sparkle has dimmed a little. My mother left a wonderful legacy for my family to live for. We still have so much fun. We try to travel when we can and of course to keep the family love strong. Mom would not want it any other way.

Connecting with Faith

After my mother was diagnosed six years ago, I investigated the Gloria Gemma Foundation and how their resources could help. She didn't want me to connect because it meant she would have to talk about it and people would see her bald head. I always told her I loved her head bald; it was beautiful. She said "I don't like it, and never will." I would just shrug my shoulders and smile at her because I knew how beautiful she was. Mom was not the type to ask for help, she was the one always helping, I believe that is why it was hard to connect with Gloria Gemma.

I've always like what Gloria Gemma Foundation had to offer. After my mother's passing, I decided to join Flames of Hope and carry a torch in my mother's memory. It was such a beautiful experience. I met beautiful people there. They made me feel at home when I arrived at the Rhode Island State House alone, a little scared because I never held a torch before. Not for long did I feel that way. The ladies in pink made me feel so welcome and I was ready to hold the torch. Finally, it was time to walk and hold the torch. My heart was racing, I kept thinking, "am I going to drop the torch and ruin things? I finally was handed the torch, my heart stopped beating fast and my thoughts were clearer. I looked out in the crowd, and I saw my family and friends; their smiles were so big, it made me feel more at ease. It was a beautiful moment, and I felt my mother's presence the entire time.

Since the Flames of Hope event, I was told about a grief group that Gloria Gemma provided. In the beginning I didn't want to attend. I did not want to talk about my mother's death or anything about her really. I didn't want to feel sad or angry thinking about her. With some convincing I finally joined and I'm so happy I did. The Grief group has provided me with support and healing, and helped me to feel better talking about my feelings and emotions without judgement. It was refreshing to chat with other people who are going through the same exact thing. Since my first meeting, I always looked forward to a session. It helps me get through my days a litter easier. I am grateful for that.

As the years went by, I saw my mother as this radiant mother nature. I always told her this, because all animals love her. Whatever pet we had in the family would be mean to us but always loved my mother. Too funny! We had this love bird called Marty, he flew on our neighbor's roof and then flew over to our house in my sister's hair. She screamed and ran with a love bird in her hair. Our family will never forget that day. My mother got the bird out of my sister's hair and the bird immediately got on my mom's shoulders like he was there from the beginning. Since that day we had the bird for about six years, he was my mother's favorite. She always enjoyed animals and flowers. She had such a warm-natured heart. I always like to share the bird memory as it's funny and sweet.

These are the memories I treasure; I had such a beautiful life with my mother, trying to live without her sometimes is hard, but doable. Some days I would not even want to get out of bed. I wanted to stay under the bed covers until someone came and got me. The struggle to get up and live life after my mother's passing was not fun. I used to say, "what is the point to get up?" I knew I had to keep going. I find myself sometimes driving and I pull over because I'm having a panic attack. When those were more frequent, I used to call my mom and she would always say comforting words to calm me down. "How am I going to get through a panic attack without her?" I did it. I calmed my own self down; I couldn't believe it. "Wait, did I just calm my own self down?" Yes, I did it without her. I've been better at controlling my attacks and anxiety. I just don't think so hard anymore about her passing and it makes it a little easier for the days ahead. She always said, "one day you will have to live without me" and I said, "what would I do?" Mom said you live a happy life like I did. Those words have stuck in my head for a long time, and they always will.

The Path She Left

A couple of years after mom's passing, our family was starting to go with the flow of life. We started to enjoy things again like going out to eat at fancy restaurants, going to Salem or even going to New York to see a play. The things we always did with Mom, we are now doing them without her, and I feel okay and not guilty. I promised my mother I didn't want to stop doing the things we loved to do. When the first thing in my mind is her or my mother-in-law, I say to myself "they should be here starting this day with me." I would scream into my pillow sometimes; I didn't know how else to express myself because I was mad at my mom. Why aren't you here with us? I didn't let this consume me; she wouldn't want that. I started to learn how to deal with my grief better by talking to her in the morning saying, "Hey, how you doing in heaven? Did you sleep on your cloud well?" I wouldn't get answers, knowing they can hear me, it's all that matters. It would make my day a little happier.

Everyone is different in how they grieve. My way is by talking to them and looking for signs around me. The path she left for us to move on is beautiful, including the lessons of love, hardships and how to deal with them. When Mom was alive, she had every obstacle hit her in the face, and she faced them with a smile. Even in the worst pain or no pain, she still had the biggest smile. Sometimes I would say "Mom, why are you smiling, aren't you in pain"? She would say "yes, but it could be worse. I'm with my family, I'll be okay." I admired her so much. Mom was the definition of a mom; kind, sweet, compassionate, and overall selfless. She always took care of others before she took care of herself. She was a beautiful soul and is missed tremendously. I hope my story helps you heal with love and light.

Joanna King

CHAPTER 10

A Mother's Love

In loving memory of Donna Parise
November 27, 1956 – November 12, 2012

By Arthur Parise Jr.

Life is full of singular moments; moments that live within us forever and change the course of our lives, unbeknownst to us at the time. We look back at these moments for guidance, wisdom, and clarity when we need it most. Often, we reflect on how our lives would have turned out if we made different choices. The decisions we make put us on a path that leads us to where we are now, where we are meant to be. Almost more importantly, the people we encounter can influence and inspire our lives. For me, one of those people was my mom. She, along with my father, loved me, nurtured me, and raised me to be the person I am today. Although I am no longer able to create memories with my mother, I always look back on the ones I was able to make and treasure them. I look back to those moments that span over the course of twenty-two years to help me navigate life and face the challenges it presents. It is easy to look at my time with my mother and think it was far too short, but in retrospect it is more than some people are given.

It has been over ten years since I lost my mother and every now and then I reflect on what she would think of the choices I made and how my life has turned out since she passed away. It is not an easy question to answer. My parents were essential in my upbringing, but every bird needs to leave the nest and fly on their own. My life can best be compared to riding a bicycle. The first twenty-two years could be considered my tricycle years. With my parents by my side, I rode through life with a bump here and there but nothing that knocked me down. But when one of those wheels was taken away unexpectedly, I struggled to stay upright and as hard as I tried, I fell down hard. However, with time and practice, I have learned to stay upright and ride through life more smoothly without falling down.

Throughout life, it is okay to make mistakes, especially when life gets bumpy but there are two crucial things to remember that I learned from my mother. The first is that when life knocks you down you get back up. My mother faced so many challenges during her battle with breast cancer. Each time she overcame an obstacle, two more would come to take its place. However, my mom was the strongest woman I have ever known and she met every challenge head on and overcame every single one until the end. The second is that when you make a mistake you learn and grow from it, continue forward, and try not to repeat it. My mother was always forgiving and understanding when I made mistakes but she raised me to not make the same mistake twice. I have scars from the mistakes that I had after she passed away and I will bear those scars for the rest of my life. They serve as reminders of my resilience and strength to overcome every obstacle that life has thrown at me. Those are qualities that I received from my mother. As I look back at everything that has happened to me the past ten years I can finally say that I am riding through life more smoothly. Although there will always be bumps in life, the big ones no longer knock me down.

My bond with my mother began on a summer afternoon on August 30th, 1990 when she gave birth to me. I was her first-born son and at that time her third child having already given birth to my two older sisters. For obvious reasons I have no recollection of that day, but I know I was brought into this world in the arms of my two loving parents and the unconditional love that they had for me. That love would continue to grow and strengthen as the years passed, although sometimes in ways we could not have anticipated. One of those ways presented itself immediately after my birth.

It is often said that immediately after having a baby most parents count their baby's fingers and toes to make sure there are ten of each. If my parents did that they would have been relieved to see that I did have all ten fingers and toes. However, they were surprised that five of my toes were on a deformed foot. My left foot was rotated inward in what is known as a club foot. Within a week, I was operated on and sent home with a baby sized leg cast. Five years later that same foot was operated on, which left me bound to a wheelchair over the course of a few months. Although not a typically normal birth, I entered this world exactly like my mother, unique and memorable. Being named after my dad, my parent's nicknamed me "Boo" due to all the other "boo boos" I would endure throughout my life.

Fourteen months later on November 12th, 1991 the last member of our family was born. My brother was the sixth member of our family and my mother's fourth child. Three years later, he was diagnosed with autism. Any parent of a child with a disability will tell you it is not easy. Raising children in general is not easy but a child with disability is a completely different experience with its own unique challenges and obstacles. It was also different back in the early 1990's and there weren't as many programs and services as there are today. Being a stay-at-home mom, my mom spent all day every day with my brother and along with my dad was his strongest advocate and made sure he received everything he needed to eventually become a successful adult. Even with all the obstacles that arose, my mom met them head on in pursuit of a better life for my brother. Anyone who has met my brother would describe him as very social with a contagious and bubbly personality. He has for over ten years held a job at BJ's Wholesale Club and I could not be more proud of the man he has become.

Growing up in my mom's house, you would notice three distinct features: a spotless home, home-cooked food, and lots of kids. These could all be attributed to my mother who, despite raising four children, would find the time to do the endless tasks that a house presents as well as raise a family. Family was everything to my mom and all the work she did, she did for us.

Like my mom, I love to clean and find it therapeutic, but she took it to a whole different level. Unlike today where people use Swiffers, Shark Vacs, and Roombas, my mom would be on her hands and knees washing the floor with nothing but a bucket and a rag. With all the foot traffic in my house from people and dogs I am still amazed how my mom always kept those floors spotless. She also had a gift of finding every cobweb and speck of dust in our house and removing any trace that it was ever there. Among other skills, my mom painted the walls and ceilings in our house, wallpapered the kitchen, and maintained her garden. As an adult I have a new appreciation of everything she did to make our home what it was and how much time and energy she sacrificed to make sure we had a home that was clean, cozy, and safe.

Another distinct feature of my childhood was the smell of my mom's home cooked food that radiated from the kitchen. I remember coming home from school and I would do my homework at the kitchen table while my mom would bake one of her mouthwatering desserts. Chocolate chip cookies, brownies, blueberry and apple squares, blondies, cheesecake, the list goes on and on. You name it, my mom could make it, and if she didn't, she would learn how to. As my siblings and I got older, my mother started to grow bored of making the same dishes and sought something challenging and started expanding beyond her usual recipes, seeking new dishes to learn how to make. I remember my first time going to Panda Express trying orange chicken for the first time. I believe that was one of the first recipes that I asked my mom if she could learn how to make. It didn't take long before my mom looked up a recipe online and my family had a bowl of orange glazed chicken on the kitchen table for dinner added into her dinner rotation. After every family dinner we had, my dad without missing a beat would always tell my mom how delicious dinner was. As a kid this seemed silly because her food was always delicious and it seemed so tedious to say the same thing every day. I just let my empty plate and mouthful of food speak for itself.

Despite raising four children, my mother had an open-door policy for all of our friends and family. It wouldn't be uncommon for all of my siblings to have friends over at the same time. My fondest childhood memories were the pool parties we had in our backyard, and sleepovers in the living room and basement. Anyone who came over would feel welcomed and loved by my mom. She made the house a home not just for her children but for anyone else who walked through the door. If you were to ask my family, they would all agree that the friends that I brought home were by far the quirkiest characters to come through our door. Nevertheless, my friendships were welcome and accepted by my mother without any judgment.

To this day I am a huge Star Wars fan, but it started when I was a five-year-old boy confined to a wheelchair with not much to do. My dad purchased the VHS tapes of the original Star Wars trilogy and from then on, I was hooked. As luck would have it my love was fueled even more with the release of a new Star Wars "prequel" trilogy that was released in 1999. As nerdy as it was, my mom not only supported my love for the galaxy far, far away, she encouraged it. On birthdays and holidays, she went on a hunt for the Star Wars items that I asked for, often losing track and purchasing an abundance of Star Wars toys. Although my mom didn't watch, know, or understand the Star Wars movies, she tried her best to find items that would bring me joy. She knew all of my siblings well, what brought us joy, and did her best to navigate the interests that we had.

There was a day in the summer of 2002 that stands out above all others as one of my fondest memories of my mother. I was eleven years old, and I had just finished my first year of middle school. On this particular day my mom took me to go shopping with her. Whether it was intentional or serendipity, I ended up purchasing the soundtrack of Star Wars Episode II Attack of the Clones that had been released in theaters earlier that year. After purchasing the soundtrack, we got into the car to go home. I hesitated to ask my mom a question that had been bouncing around in my head since purchasing the soundtrack. After going back and forth in my head contemplating on whether I should ask or not I blurted out, "Can we listen to the CD now please?" To my surprise and delight my mom smiled and agreed. I scrambled to remove the plastic wrap from the case and fumbled with the disc in excitement. As the CD was inserted into the car, there were a few seconds of silence as I waited for the first track to be played. Suddenly, it exploded with John William's famous Star Wars opening theme. Looking back driving with my mom in her convertible blasting the Star Wars soundtrack is one of my fondest memories with her. I don't know how many moms would blast the Star Wars soundtrack for their kid, I just know that mine did. Twenty years later I still listen to that soundtrack and smile remembering that special day.

Parents are supposed to love their kids unconditionally. However, the sad truth is that sometimes that love is tested and shaken to its core and the outcome isn't what one would hope for. In the spring of 2006, I was just finishing my sophomore year of high school. On one particular day I was in the living room with my mom watching television. I don't remember what we were watching because of the fact that I wasn't paying any attention to it. I was sitting there nervous, my heart pounding, my body shaking, and my brain trying to muster the strength to say something that I had been holding back for years. As the minutes passed, I reached down for all the courage for this monumental moment. Amidst the unstructured and spontaneous mess of words I was spewing from my mouth there were two that stood out amongst the others. "I'm gay," I said. My heart stopped, all of the air in my lungs was released and in that moment time stood still. Whether it was ten seconds or ten minutes time was irrelevant; in that moment the only thing that mattered was what my mom did next. There were two things following my confession that my mom said. The first was she asked me if I was sure. I had known for years that I was gay and could no longer continue to live a lie and deny myself of being who I was. Her question was not based on any negative thoughts or opinions on my sexuality. She just knew that living a life as an openly gay man would not always be easy. She just wanted me to be happy and safe as I navigated this new stage of my life. The second thing she said was that she loved me. As I exhaled a breath that I had been unintentionally holding, I felt the weight of the world finally lifted off my shoulders. Over the course of the coming weeks my mom helped me come out to the rest of my family. Finally, after years of uncertainty, I was out, I was proud, and I was supported. What more could I ask for? I had just confronted the hardest part of my teenage years; I was certain that the rest would be a breeze. Little did I know, I couldn't have been more wrong.

In the fall of that same year I was just starting my junior year in high school and things in my life were going relatively well. I was out with nothing but support and acceptance from friends and family. I was doing well in school, living my best life. Suddenly something happened that would change the course of my life forever and shake my family to its core. One night before dinner, my parents called my siblings and I into their bedroom to talk about something. This was very unusual and I would be lying if I said I wasn't a little nervous. This was not something that had ever happened before, and I knew that whatever it was about could not be good. As we all sat on the bed, that is when my parents told us something that none of us had ever expected to hear. My mother had recently been diagnosed with breast cancer and she would soon be getting a double mastectomy to remove the cancer. The room was so silent all I could hear was my heart pounding. Although I don't remember much from that day, I do remember my immediate response. "What's for dinner?" The once silent room was now filled with smirks. Humor is a very strong quality that was fostered in my family. To anyone else, my comment might seem like an insensitive response. However, my parents knew that was my way of saying that everything was going to be okay and that I wasn't worried. The truth is that deep down I was terrified of what the future would hold. Would she be okay? Would she die? The number of questions racing through my head was immeasurable. But I did not want my mom to see my worry, I wanted to be strong for her for I knew whatever I was feeling, she was going through something far worse. My mom assured us that everything would be alright, but I was left pondering a thought. Was everything really going to be alright or was she trying to be strong for us? The next couple of years were tough for my mother. Looking back now, after that night sitting on my parents' bed, things would never be the same. Although I still had my mother, I truly did lose a piece of her that day.

As the months went forward, my mother had her ups and downs with her health. She would not end up seeing me walk the stage when I graduated high school in the spring of 2008 due to her health. Soon after, I would attend Rhode Island College to work towards my teaching degree. Over the next few years, I made very special memories with my mother that I would not trade for anything. I came home every weekend to see my parents (and do laundry). I started to run in the Gloria Gemma 5K races to show support for my mother. I couldn't take away all the pain and suffering she had gone through. However, she inspired me to run for her and those who no longer could. Running into her warm embrace was the best feeling in the world for both of us.

There is never a right time or way to lose a parent or someone close to you. Sometimes you know it is coming and sometimes it is unexpected and takes you by surprise. In regard to my mother it was the latter. My last memories of her were during my last year of college in the fall of 2011. I remember coming home one Wednesday night and watching TV with her and, before I went to bed, I told her that I loved her. Unbeknownst to me at the time that would be the last words I ever said to her. The next night on Thursday I came home, but she was already in bed because she was not feeling well. Friday night, I ended up working late and by the time I came home she was already in bed. Saturday morning I woke up to my dad screaming my name and my mom leaving by ambulance. I won't go into details out of respect for my mom and my family, but the short story is that two days later she passed away.

However sad as I was, I remember also feeling a sense of relief. My mom was no longer in pain, and she no longer suffered. Finally, after many years, she was at peace. The following week was by far the worst week of my life as well as my whole family's. I went through the next few days numb and emotionless, unable to experience any happiness. I had just unexpectedly lost one of the people I love most in this world. There honestly is no right time or circumstance in which one is ready to lose someone they love. I can personally say that I was severely not prepared to lose my mom. To lose her unexpectedly was like having the wind knocked out of me. There is one moment in the days that followed that I had a brief moment of happiness and it came from somewhere completely unexpected, my mother.

For years my mom and I played Words with Friends together and although she was good at the game, she would more often than not lose to me. Not because I had a huge vocabulary but because I was strategic and used words that I made up to see if they were real. I would often laugh over her frustration at losing. Before my mom passed, we had been playing a game and I was in the lead. My mother and I had a playful competitive nature and the day of her funeral I approached the casket, gave her a kiss, said my last goodbye and whispered "I won" to her. A fitting goodbye for the competitive relationship we had. The days that followed I kept getting notifications from Words with Friends that it was my turn. With grief still present, I didn't have the heart to touch the game, nor was there any reason to continue it. It wasn't long until I got another notification for Words with Friends. It turns out that after a certain amount of time, if you don't go when it is your turn, the game ends and your opponent automatically wins the game. Due to this, it turns out that my mom won the game. As I read the notification, I smiled for the first time that week. Touché Mom, touché. The following spring, I graduated college with my teaching degree. Although my mom was not there to watch me walk the stage, I had a picture of her on my cap.

In the years that passed since my mother passed away, I became a shell of my former self. I buried myself in work and avoided the pain of the loss of losing my mom. With college finished I moved home. I started to teach full time as well as work part time with kids with disabilities as a PASS (personal assistance services and supports) worker. I stepped into my mom's shoes and made sure the house was clean, I learned to cook and made dinner every night and made sure my brother's life was as unchanged as I could make possible. I remember one of the first meals I made dinner for my dad and brother was meatloaf. I had accidentally misread a teaspoon as a tablespoon and ended up putting an abundance of pepper into the recipe. The meatloaf was too spicy and required a waterfall of ketchup to be somewhat edible. However, my dad repeated the phrase that he used to say to my mother and told me it was good. It wasn't until then that I finally understood why he would tell my mother that every night she cooked. He knew how hard I tried and that was him supporting me. As time went on, I navigated the learning curves and soon was making the same dishes that I grew up eating.

Not long after my mom passed, my sister got engaged and married the love of her life. They have had two children together and one of my greatest joys in life has been watching her become a mother. My siblings and I have all inherited qualities and traits from our parents, but watching my sister become a wife and mother is like looking at a younger version of Mother. My sister has all the qualities and traits of our mother and in the past seven years I have never been more proud of her. She is a great mother and she is instilling in her kids the same childhood and upbringing our mother gave us. I know that if my mom were alive today, she would be proud of the woman she has become, and she would have loved her grandchildren with all of her heart.

Although life was moving on and our family was happily expanding, I was not happy. Ignoring my feelings and pushing away my grief did not make them go away as much as I tried to convince myself otherwise. It didn't take long before I found myself doing things I never would have done before and put myself in situations I never would have imagined. One such situation put me face to face with an individual who had also lost his mother. In this particular situation, I came face to face with my first interaction with an illegal addictive drug. This is a situation I should never have put myself in. Years ago, I would have said no and left and never looked back, but in that moment amidst my depression, sadness, and grief I said yes and lit up the pipe.

The world is not something you can simply compartmentalize. Things aren't always black and white, people aren't inherently good or evil and there aren't simply two sides to a story. We live in a world that is complicated and rapidly changing. For the purpose of this discussion, I would like to picture a line. On one side you have people who have never done drugs, and on the other you have people who became addicted to drugs and whose lives fall apart because of them. If you were to place me using this visual, you would find me standing directly on the line. I was living right on the edge; stray but a little and my life could have been brought back to who I was or plunge into further chaos.

I lived on that line for years until finally I decided to finally pick a side and commit to it. My grief had snowballed into something mean and unrecognizable. I lied, cheated, and put myself in situations that could have ended in jail or death. I had strayed from the path my mom left me and ceased to be who I was. I didn't know where I was or where I was going but I knew it wouldn't end well if I didn't make a change. For the second time in my life, I had a "coming out" moment where I had to share a deep secret to those close to me. However, this time was different. I didn't have my mom to go to, she couldn't help me this time. I had to use a life's worth of wisdom, lessons, and skills to carefully maneuver how my future would unfold. I was at that time a shell of my former self. But when the shell fails, the essence remains.

Do you remember how you felt as a kid when you found yourself all alone in the pitch darkness, unable to see anything? That is what it felt like when I lost my mom. I was scared, confused, and unable to see what the future would hold. Even in my darkest time, hope remained. In that darkness, the Gloria Gemma Foundation was the spark that helped me find the light. I started to mourn and perhaps more importantly, I started to heal. In the last ten years I have walked a total of over three hundred miles in Gloridays, a three day, forty-four mile walk to support those who are affected by breast cancer and to honor those who have passed. I watch other mothers walk with their sons, and I know that my role has now changed. I walk to honor my mother but now my path has changed. I will continue what started with my mother. I will always remember and walk for my mother. Now however I continue my work to help other mothers so that they can have those with their children that I can no longer have with mine.

Through Gloria Gemma I found hope, hope that things will get better, and they have. Today I am in a much better place. With the support of my family and friends I am back to the person I once was. With the support of the Gloria Gemma Breast Cancer Foundation, I have faced the grief of my loss, and have moved forward with my life. I no longer mourn the time that was taken from me but treasure the extra time I was given. From my mom's diagnosis until her passing I was given an additional four years.

In those four years I graduated high school, entered my last year of college in the pursuit of a teaching degree and grew to a man that my mom would be proud of. Currently, I teach kindergarten special education, my relationship with my dad and siblings is strong and I am a proud guncle (gay uncle) to my niece and nephew. I also have a loving and supportive boyfriend who has supported me in my involvement with the Gloria Gemma Breast Cancer Foundation. He has even twice participated in Gloridays with me. I feel more like myself than I have in a long time. Grief and loss can shake you to your core and turn your life upside down. When things seem darkest, there is always hope.

There is a quote I turn to when times get tough that I hope brings some sort of comfort to those who know the pain of loss. "Our parents die, our teachers die. The losses in life's long journey are great. The first reaction is often 'I can't make it with this, help.' But it is crucial that the help not stay. That they either leave or die, or we would never know that we have taken in the teachings. The mentor is now within, and I am able to survive. As valuable as the mentor relationship is, ultimately we will outlive it." As I look back at everything my mom taught me, I know she will always be with me. As a wise Jedi master once said, "no one is ever really gone."

Arthur Parise Jr. & Donna Parise

About Susan Lataille

Susan Lataille has had her own experience with grief after the loss of her only son in 2017. She knows first hand that grieving is a process that can take you by storm and impact every part of your life. She has found hope and inspiration through others' stories and wants you to as well. She has found her purpose in life in helping others with their grieving process through her unique process.

Working with the ten authors of this book has given her the vantage point of watching each one grow and process layers of their grief. It was truly an honor to be given the opportunity to offer this project to such an amazing organization.

Susan Lataille is a Certified Master Grief Coach assisting others along their grief journey through her "Shining a Light on Grief" anthology series, individual and group coaching sessions, workshops, and retreats. She is also a HeartMath® Certified Mentor, Certified International Nutritional Health Coach, Reiki Master, and more.

Email: susan@susanlataille.com
Website: www.shiningalightongrief.com

www.ingramcontent.com/pod-product-compliance
Lightning Source LLC
Chambersburg PA
CBHW071116160426
43196CB00013B/2583